ALPHA T

The A – Z of Teaching
Reading, Writing and Spelling

3rd Edition

by

BEVE HORNSBY, M.Sc, M.Ed., L.C.S.T.
Head of Dyslexia Clinic,
St. Bartholomew's Hospital, London

and

FRULA SHEAR, J.P.
Language Therapist,
St. Bartholemew's Hospital, and formerly
Westminster Children's Hospital, London

HEINEMANN
LONDON

comparison
Comparative

Heinemann Educational Books Ltd
22 Bedford Square, London WC1B 3HH

LONDON EDINBURGH MELBOURNE AUCKLAND
HONG KONG SINGAPORE KUALA LUMPUR NEW DELHI
IBADAN NAIROBI JOHANNESBURG
EXETER (NH) KINGSTON PORT OF SPAIN

ISBN 0 435 10382 2

Typeset by The Castlefield Press of High Wycombe
in 11/15pt Journal Roman, and printed in Great Britain
by Biddles of Guildford

Preface and Acknowledgements

The roots of the ideas that form the basis of this programme lie in the work of Anne Gillingham and Bessie Stillman, who, in conjunction with Samuel T. Orton, began to devise a phonetically based scheme for the teaching of dyslexics in the 1930s. This was later expounded in this country by Sally B. Childs.

At approximately the same time Edith Norrie, a speech therapist and herself a dyslexic, began to realise the value of phonetics in the teaching of those with a specific reading and spelling difficulty and produced her letter case.

Although acknowledgements are freely given to their work and its influence on the present authors' efforts, and also to Miss Holt of the Wordblind Clinic at Bart's whose first trainee one of us (BH) was, the following programme has been built up over four years of clinical observation of what it is that the dyslexic finds so difficult and training and shaping these weaknesses so that they are overcome.

We would also like to thank Columbia University for the use of the *Thorndike Lorge Word List*. For permission to quote from simplified editions we thank Messrs Longman (*Pickwick Papers*) and Messrs Longman and Johathan Cape (*The Caine Mutiny*).

Finally, we are grateful to all those who combed through the text of the original, experimental edition for errors and omissions.

We hope you will find this book useful.

Preface to Third Edition

The alterations, corrections and omissions in this third edition
are the result of suggestions and criticisms from many sources. It
has proved impossible to include, or delete, everything suggested.
We have, therefore, tried to keep an even balance.

Three spelling tests have been added at the end of each stage in
order to test the student's ability at various stages of development.

Further cross references have been added to the index.

Our thanks are due to all who have made suggestions, some of
which we have incorporated.

NOTE

A set of *Flashcards* (ISBN 0 435 10381 4) is now available for
use with this book (see pages 13 and 18 for suggested application).
The cards, supplied in a strong cardboard box, cover vowels,
single letters and sounds, consonant digraphs, consonant blends,
vowel/consonant digraphs, 'magic e', hard or soft c and g, vowel
digraphs, open and closed syllables, and useful social vocabulary.

The *Flashcards* may be ordered through your usual supplier or,
in case of difficulty, from the publishers.

Dedicated to the memory of

JACK MYDDLETON HORNSBY

without whose support and encouragement
we might never have completed

Alpha to Omega

Contents

LIST OF ODD WORDS

Foreword

This is a phonetic, linguistic approach to the teaching of reading, writing and spelling. Phonetics is the scientific study of speech sounds and linguistics is the scientific study of language. It is considered necessary to have a thorough knowledge of these subjects in order to teach a language skill.

With an ever-increasing emphasis on education and literacy, more and more children and adults are asking for and needing help in learning to read. Reading is the problem usually mentioned but, of course, this is but one aspect of general language ability. There is a widespread tendency to concentrate on getting people to read and to neglect both the ability for verbal expression and the ability to put words on paper, that is to say, spelling. As the use of speech, the ability to read the printed word and the ability to write down words are all part of language ability as a whole, all these areas should be taught and improved concurrently. Learning and practice in any one of these three skills will increase the pupil's understanding and experience of language as a whole and will thus help in the other spheres too. To be able to read but not write reasonably coherent English with satisfactory spelling, will not get anyone far in our present educational system and competitive employment world.

It is on these lines then, that the following programme has been devised.

Dr. Sonia Machanick, M.B., Ch.B.

The Key

My boy sits
Curled over
The book,
Holding it
Too tightly
With a thin hand
And
Tense in his uncertainty.

My boy looks
Seeing black
Symbols
And
Something close
To loathing
Saps his concentration.

To me
The words unlock
A store of vast delight,
But my boy
Does not have
The key.

By kind permission of
J. Brunskill-Davis, L.C.S.T.
Speech Therapist.

Teacher's Guide

Although this programme has been designed specifically for dyslexics (or reading retardates, whichever term is preferred) it is
felt that it might be equally useful for all backward readers, or for
foreigners learning English, since written language is certainly a
foreign language to the dyslexic. In fact, it's all Greek to him!
It has had to be made appropriate, therefore, to a very wide age
range, from the seven-year-old to people of forty or more.

*It must, obviously then, be left to the discretion
of the teacher to choose those words, exercises,
sentences and games which are appropriate to the
age and interests of the student concerned.*

It is a highly structured programme, which has been found by
experience in the teaching of language skills to all delayed or
disordered language groups (including aphasics and autistics) to
be far more effective than a random one.

The structure closely follows the normal pattern of phonological and language acquisition; each step leads naturally and
logically one into the other, and at no point is the pupil required
to read or write any spelling pattern or language structure which
has not been specifically taught. Therefore, everything he is asked
to do is completely comprehensible, failure is eliminated and
errorless learning takes place.

Obviously, it is not possible to explain everything, or the book
would become a tome and defeat its object of lightness and
simplicity. It is assumed then, that the teacher has an adequate
knowledge of English grammar and syntax, and it is recommended
he or she take a course in phonetics and linguistics so that the
sound patterns of the English language are fully understood and
correctly taught. (Letter sounds should not be given an added
schwa, or unstressed /er/ sound, for instance.)

We begin, as does the infant, with phonological acquisition
(babbling patterns) and learn the sound patterns which have to be
associated with the letters of the Roman Alphabet, hence the title

Alpha to Omega or A to Z as the Roman Alphabet was originally adapted from the Greek. These letters represent the symbols by which spoken language is translated into written language. They are first acquired in a one to one relationship — one phoneme, one grapheme (one sound, one letter). This is gradually built up to encompass all the possible combinations of letters required to produce 44 phonemes from the 26 available letters. It is from these 44 phonemes that all English words are composed. There are 17 vowel sounds and 27 consonants.

TABLE 1

Order of consonants normally acquired:—

1	b p m w h
2	d t n g k /ŋ/ (ng)
3	f s z
4	v TH (voiced/ð/) sh /ʒ/ l ch j
5	y qu /kw/ r th /θ/ x /ks/ or /gz/
6	Consonant blends

The phonetic symbol /ʒ/ cannot be represented in traditional orthography, but is the medial sound in 'tre<u>a</u>s<u>u</u>re', and is a voiced /sh/.

These consonant sounds usually appear first in the initial position, then the medial and then the final. It follows that consonants in the final position are found to be the most difficult to distinguish by disabled readers, particularly between the voiced and voiceless pairs such as /t/ and /d/, the placing of the nasals /m/ and /n/, and the manner in which sounds are made, such as the distinction between the fricative /sh/ and the affricate /ch/. Much discrimination work is needed therefore on these sounds.

The sounds should be taught in the order in which they appear, finishing with the consonant blends which usually present much difficulty, both initially and finally.

Of the vowels, only their names (which are also their long sounds) and their short sounds are taught to begin with. These are the five vowels a e i o u. The rest of the vowel sounds are introduced gradually through Stages I and II.

When teaching the short sounds of the five vowels it is as well to bear in mind the placing of these sounds in the mouth (all vowels are voiced), and choose those which are as far apart as possible, to make discrimination less difficult. Thus /ă/ and /ŏ/ are a good pair to contrast, then /ĭ/ and /ŭ/ and finally /ĕ/ when the others are firmly established. The ones that are constantly confused for obvious reasons (see table below) are /ĕ/ and /ă/.

TABLE 2

Placement of the five short vowels

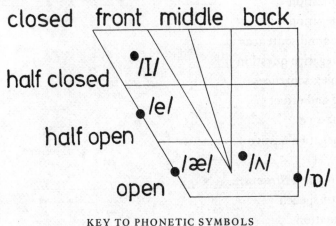

KEY TO PHONETIC SYMBOLS

/I/ as in bid /e/ as in bed
/æ/ as in bad /ʌ/ as in bud
/ɒ/ as in pod

Similarly, *language structure* follows the normal pattern of language acquisition. Content words appear first — nouns, verbs and adjectives — while function words (the 'little' words: prepositions, particles etc.) appear last. Hence the 'telegrammatic' speech of the infant (and the aphasic) and the leaving out of the 'little' words in the dyslexic's written work.

As soon as the pupil is able to synthesise sounds into words and analyse words into their component parts, these words are used in sentences. In the same way that a phoneme has no meaning until used in context in a word, a word has no real meaning until used in context in a sentence.

These sentences are SAAD sentences to begin with. SAAD sentences (Simple Active Affirmative Declarative) are considered by Noam Chomsky to be the universal deep structure of all languages. They are certainly the first type of sentences to be produced by the child. These sentences are then subjected to transformations, firstly in sentences given for dictation and later the pupil is asked to make them for himself. They are taught in the following order:—
The SAAD sentence
The question
The negation
Compound sentences
The negative question
Complex sentences
Cause and effect
The passive
The negative passive

Grammatical Structure:—
Parts of speech
Punctuation
Tense
Personal pronoun replacement
Possessive pronoun replacement
Relative pronoun replacement
'Wh' words
Shortened forms
Dialogue
Reported speech

Different registers – informal, formal
Précis
Note taking
Essay writing
Writing learned papers

Diacritical marks:–
These are similar to those used in *Chambers Twentieth Century Dictionary.*
Short vowels ˘/ă/ as in hat (breve)
Long vowels ¯/ā/ as in hate (macron)
Digraphs ⁀ t͡h o͡r o͡w
Stress but′ter
Syllable division /but/ter
Schwa (unstressed /er/ sound) /ə/

TH	the voiced 'th' as in then /ð/
zh	the voiced 'sh' as in plea_s_ure /ʒ/
gz	the voiced 'x' as in _e_xample /gz/
ng	the velarised 'n' as in bang /ŋ/
ngg	the 'ng' and 'g' as in finger /ŋg/
ngk	the 'nk' sound as in bank /ŋk/

Letters or letter names are given in inverted commas 'a'
Sounds of letters or groups of letters are given in slanted brackets /a/

The words used have been taken from the *Thorndike/Lorge Teacher's Word List of 30,000 Words* which lists words according to the frequency with which they are used. The most frequent are AA words, then A words then down from 50 to 1.

In general, only words with a frequency count of more than 10 have been used in this scheme, but in certain cases the frequency count is given so that the teacher can use discretion as to which words to give the pupil, according to his age, intelligence, cultural background and aspirations.

A *digraph* means *two letters* giving *one sound*. This term is used throughout where two letters give one sound, regardless of whether the letters are vowels or consonants. It must be understood that a *consonant blend* is not a *digraph* since each letter retains its separate sound, although we teach blends as complete units.

Type of letters
It must be understood that there are two processes involved here — reading and writing — thus all letters presented for reading, that is, for translation from written symbol to sound, will be lower case printing (Times Print for preference) or manuscript. Always teach lower case letters before capitals, otherwise capitals will be constantly inappropriately used, and it is a habit which is very difficult to lose.

Handwriting
Before embarking on writing, or remediation of a writing problem, the child needs to know the letter name, its sound, and recognise its shape. The writing of numbers and punctuation should be checked.

A cursive script is preferable, i.e. all letters which end on the base line are taught with an appropriate ligature (joining stroke). As soon as a child is capable of writing all the letters correctly, then the joining up of letters should be encouraged. Our occupational therapist has devised a tracing and copying writing programme which closely follows the spelling patterns used in *Alpha to Omega*. All letters should be first referred to by their names. Lower case letters should be taught first, capital letters being introduced when necessary.

The pupil should be seated at a table and chair of correct height so that his feet rest flat on the floor. The paper should be slanted to the left for a right handed writer and to the right for left handers. The free hand should be placed on the paper and the pencil supported lightly in a tripod grip. Plastic pencil grips are available to facilitate a good pencil hold.

Writing is for Reading
by Jane Taylor M.B.A.O.T. Dip. Ed.
Occupational Therapist

Summary of the Programme

Stage I
This stage deals with one syllable words, except where prefixes and suffixes can be added without changing the spelling of the 'root' word.

The vowels are mostly short vowels, or one and two phoneme words ending in a vowel — these are open syllable words and the vowel will, therefore, be long. For example:—

ā	bē	hē	mē	shē	thē	wē
	nō	sō	go	tō	dō	
	Ī	bȳ	mȳ			

We also use 'lengthening e' long vowels, which are really a re-opening of the syllable:—

cake   these   ripe   hope   tune

Stage II
This stage also deals with one syllable words but now we add prefixes and suffixes where the final spelling of the 'root' word *does* change. Here we also discover the other ways of getting long vowels.

Stage III
This stage deals with polysyllabic words; the peculiarities of final syllables and the open and closed syllable is gone into more thoroughly.

All instructions must, of course, be read to the pupil, and if necessary explained.

Prefixes and Suffixes
A prefix is a morpheme placed in front of a word to change or extend its meaning. A suffix is a morpheme placed after a word to change its function.

Those it is felt must be mastered are:—

PREFIXES			SUFFIXES		
a	be	de	ed	er	est
en	mis	in	ing	ous	able
re	to	un	ly	s	ment
ad	dis	pre	y	age	ful

More advanced prefixes and suffixes are introduced later, or form part of some rule being taught.

Games and exercises can be devised to help the pupil become familiar with the concept of suffixing and prefixing. Even quite young pupils can be shown the concept using a familiar word, e.g. root word — 'do'; add prefix, 'un' = 'undo' i.e. change of *meaning* root word — 'do'; add suffix, 'ing' = 'doing' i.e. change of *function* or *tense*.

Other devices such as *Flashcards* with the root word, suffix or prefix can be incorporated into games and exercises.

Understanding prefixes and suffixes will also aid reading comprehension in later lessons.

Suggested Lesson Plan

1. Check homework and discuss any errors of spelling, punctuation or language structure that may have occurred, encouraging the pupil to discover the errors for himself and the logic underlying their correction.

2. Present the *Flashcards* of the sounds learnt to date as a 'timed' game. If the pupil is still unsure of any of them, or the teacher is presenting a new sound, use the format laid down in "Drill for Teaching Letters and Their Sounds".

3 Teach new sound or spelling pattern if the previous ones have been fully mastered. If not, revise, as one must never go on if the foundations are shaky!

4 Make words (from Letter Case), read words and write words in the new pattern, then dictate them in sentences, using the "Drill for Sentence Dictation". At this point pupils can also practise transformations as suggested in the exercises given with each new pattern.

5. Reading aloud, using "Drill for Reading".
6. Alphabet or dictionary work.
7. Game — reinforcing the work done in the lesson, correcting directional confusion or improving sequencing ability or visual imagery and memory.
8. Set new work for homework.
9. Occasionally vary this by reading *to* pupil.

The sentences, exercises, games and transformations given after each stage are only suggestions. The teacher's discretion is needed as to their suitability. Younger pupils enjoy games and benefit from the relaxing atmosphere they engender, while older students want more solid spelling and reading practice.

Reading aloud forms an essential part of each lesson but, again, the reading material must be chosen by the teacher according to the age, interests and reading age of the subject concerned. An appendix is provided giving suggestions for suitable reading matter.

Drill for Reading

Since reading usually outstrips spelling, as soon as the pupil has progressed beyond totally regular phonetic reading, the sound patterns not yet encountered in spelling should be pointed out. From these clues the pupil should be encouraged to work out the word for himself. Thus, not only is 'word attack' skill fostered but when these patterns are taught for spelling they are already half learnt. Syllable division should also be encouraged, paying particular attention to the first syllable since the stress is usually on this syllable in English. Also, if the vowel is short the syllable should be closed by a consonant, whereas if it is long the syllable should be left open. Of course, if the word is an 'Odd Word' which has not yet been taught it must be supplied at once. Attention should be paid to punctuation and expression.

Stage I

Each letter has a *name* and a *sound*.
Do you know the *names* of these letters?

a c g j m p r t w z
b d f i l o q s v
y e h k n u x

Now recite them in their alphabetical order.

Alphabet game I
When the pupil can recite the alphabet, recite it with him alternating the letters. Then try saying three letters each. Next, the teacher says two letters and the pupil three. Now the teacher recites the alphabet missing out one letter. The pupil is asked to name the missing letter. If he cannot do this, recite the alphabet slowly asking him to stop the teacher when the missing letter is reached.

Sequencing

Can you recite the days of the week? Day means the time when the sun is shining.

Monday	Moon's day.
Tuesday	Mars' day, God of war. *Twi – Twi's day*
Wednesday	Woden's day, or Jupiter's day.
Thursday	Thor's day, God of thunder.

Friday	Frig's day, or Juno's day.
Saturday	Saturn's day.
Sunday	Sun's day.

Can you recite the months of the year?
A month is a measure of time.

January	month of Janus, a Roman god.
February	month of Februa, Roman festival.
March	month of Mars.
April	possibly from Latin 'aperio'.
May	Maia, Roman Goddess of increase.
June	named after Junius, Roman family.
July	named after Julius Caesar.
August	named after Augustus Caesar.

September, October, November and December are named after the 7th, 8th, 9th and 10th months of the Roman calendar.

Do you know the names of the seasons?

Winter   Spring   Summer   Autumn

Appendix III
    Days of the week rhymes.
    Months of the year rhymes.

Can you tell the time?

Do you know?
Your address, your telephone number and your birthday.

There are 60 seconds in a minute.

There are 60 minutes in an hour.

There are 24 hours in a day.

There are 7 days in a week.

There are 52 weeks in a year.

There are 12 months in a year.

There are 365¼ days in a year.

How many days in a month?

30 days in September, April, June and November
All the rest have 31, except for February alone
      Which has 28 days clear
      And 29 in each leap year.

Now find out:—

1. How many times does the big hand go round the clock face in an hour?
2. How many times does it go round in a day?
3. How many times does the little hand go round in a day?
4. How many pence in a pound?
5. What is the highest place on earth?
6. The names of the five continents?
7. The names of the five oceans?
8. Where does the sun rise and set?
9. Do you know the points of the compass?

The Sounds of the Letters of the Alphabet

Drill for Teaching Letter/Sound Association

1. Teacher presents letter written on flashcard with key picture drawn on reverse side, pupil says letter's *name*.
2. Teacher says the key word and then the *sound* of the letter.
3. Pupil repeats key word and sound.
4. Teacher says the sound and then the *name*.
5. Pupil repeats the sound and gives the name, writing it as he says it (translating sound heard into letters written).
6. Pupil reads what he has written giving the *sound* (translating letters written into sounds heard).
7. Pupil writes letter with eyes closed to get the *feel* of the letter.
This last step is to enhance kinaesthetic feedback when the visual channel is cut out. Vision is the most powerful of the senses in humans, and tends to mask the other input channels, such as hearing and touch, unless it is cut off.

Sounds of the Letters with 'Key' Picture

Name		Sound	Name		Sound
'a'		/a/	'n'		/n/
'b'		/b/	'o'		/o/
'c'		/k/	'p'		/p/
'd'		/d/	'q' (qu)		/kw/
'e'		/e/	'r'		/r/
'f'		/f/	's'		/s/ /z/
'g'		/g/	't'		/t/
'h'		/h/	'u'		/u/
'i'		/i/	'v'		/v/
'j'		/j/	'w'		/w/
'k'		/k/	'-x'		/ks/ /gz/
'l'		/l/	'y'		/y/
'm'		/m/	'z'		/z/

— 16 —

At all times the teacher must ensure that letters are started and finished correctly, if necessary by drawing arrows for the pupil to follow.

'Key' word unlocks sound.

Consonant Digraphs

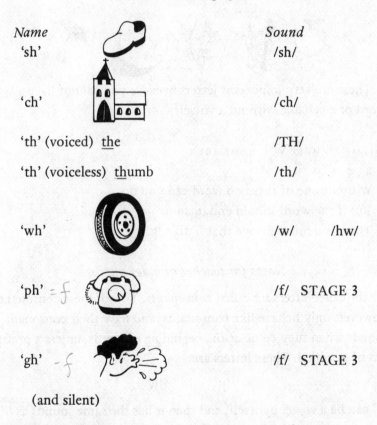

Name		Sound
'sh'		/sh/
'ch'		/ch/
'th' (voiced) <u>the</u>		/TH/
'th' (voiceless) <u>th</u>umb		/th/
'wh'		/w/ /hw/
'ph' = f		/f/ STAGE 3
'gh' -f		/f/ STAGE 3

(and silent)

It will be noticed that all *consonant* digraphs contain an 'h'. The 'wh' digraph is not usually given its /hw/ sound except in Scottish English, and 'ph' and 'gh' are taught later.

VOWELS

There are only five true vowels.

Their *names* are:—

a   e   i   o   ū

and their *short* sounds are:—

/ă/   /ĕ/   /ĭ/   /ŏ/   /ŭ/

These are very important letters because you cannot have a word or a syllable without a vowel.

RHYME TO HELP YOU REMEMBER

ā ē ī ō ū

Without one of these no word can you do,
But if the word should end in an 'i'
Then you must change that 'i' to a 'y'.

Notes for teacher or older pupils

All the other letters are called *consonants*. Two of these consonants, however, only behave like consonants, and have their consonant sounds when they come at the beginning of words, unless a prefix has been added. These letters are:—

'y'   'w'

'y' can be a vowel by itself, and then it has the same sounds as 'i'. It is always used at the ends of words instead of 'i' because English words do not end in this letter. 'w' cannot be a vowel by itself; it always joins with other vowels to form vowel digraphs:—

e.g. slow, now, few, saw.

These digraphs are taught later in the programme though, so we do not have to worry about 'w' as a vowel at this stage.

These two letters are, however, known as semi-vowels, as they are half vowels. Perhaps 'w' should be called a semi-demi-vowel? Half of half a vowel?

Remember that if the word ends in a vowel, the vowel will be *long*, that is, it will say its *name*. This is because it is an *open syllable* word. *Short* vowels are only used in *closed syllable* words (at this stage) that is, words ending in a consonant.

The letter 'c' always says /k/ at this stage, and until you are told differently, the sound /k/ is spelt with a 'c' at the beginning of a word and a 'k' at the end of a word.

You can now make a great many words using the sounds you have learnt, and some examples are given on the following page listed under their vowel sound.

Remember you can also make these *long* vowel words:—

a	be	he	me	she	the	we
	no	so	go	to	do	
	I	by	my			

When 'I' comes by itself, it must be spelt 'I' and not 'y' because it is at both the start and end of the word and would say /y/.

Short Vowel Words to Make

/ă/	/ĕ/	/ĭ/	/ŏ/	/ŭ/
bad	bed	did	hop	up
Dad	fed	hid	lop	cup
had	led	lid	mop	pup
mad	Ned	big	pop	but
pad	Ted	dig	top	cut
sad	wed	fig	bog	gut
ham	Ben	jig	dog	hut
jam	hen	pig	fog	jut
Pam	ten	wig	log	mut
Sam	men	bin	got	nut
can	get	din	hot	Mum

/ă/	/ĕ/	/ĭ/	/ŏ/	/ŭ/
fan	jet	fin	lot	hum
man	let	pin	rot	rum
Nan	net	sin	tot	sum
pan	pet	tin	cot	bun
ran	set	win	jot	fun
cap	wet	it	not	gun
tap	yet	bit	pot	run
map	beg	fit	on	sun
at	let	hit	Ron	us
bat	Meg	lit	box	bus
cat	peg	pit	fox	lux
fat	yes	sit	cod	bug
hat	bet	wit	rod	hug
sat	met	is	nod	mug

We are now going to make some sentences using those sorts of words. In the same way that every word must have a *vowel*, every sentence must have a *verb*. A verb is a doing word, and a noun is a naming word.

All sentences begin with a CAPITAL letter and end with a full stop.

When you have written these sentences, read them and underline the *nouns* and *verbs*.

(Note for teacher — all these sentences are SAAD sentences):—

SENTENCES FOR DICTATION

Tom ran to the red van.

The pan is hot.

Fat Dan cannot get in the van.

Pam can get me a pot of jam.

Len hit Ben on the chin.

Then Ben hit Len on the shin.

Sam sat in the sun to get a tan.

Rex has a big bun.

The dog can beg.
Meg and Pat can fit Sam in.
Ron met Ted on the bus.
Mum hid the pot of jam.
Dan has a gun.
Mum has a wig.
Len has a rat.

Drill for Dictation

1. Dictate whole sentence.
2. Call upon pupil to repeat it.
3. Dictate it again, saying each word very clearly, pronouncing each word as it is going to be *written* (making the translation from spoken to written language).
4. Pupil writes the sentence saying it *clearly* as he writes it (he is now making the translation from spoken to written language for himself).
5. Pupil is asked to read aloud *exactly* what he has written.
6. Final corrections are *suggested* if the pupil has failed to discover them for himself. He is never *told* what he should have written, only led by appropriate clues to *find out for himself*.

Now some more sentences, bringing in the suffix 's', the comma, (compound sentences) and the question (these two are the first of the transformations). A question ends in a question mark instead of a full stop.

SENTENCES
Pam has a lot of pins.
Ted has six hens.
I bet Tom is top of the pops.
Ben can dig, but Len cannot.
Sam cut the logs.
Pam and Meg got a fat cat to sit on the mat.
Mum got a lot of buns.

It is fun to run in the sun.
Dan got a cod in his big net.
Dad has a tot of rum and a fag.
Mum has a box of pegs.
Has Pam got a bag of pegs?
Dan has a pet dog and a hen.
The dog bit Dan, so Dan hit the dog.
Len pats his dog.
Dan pets his cat.
The dog sits and begs.
Sam hugs Meg.
Pam is so hot she puts the fan on.
Has Tom got a map, so we can get to the spot?
It is bad for that dog to be so fat.
Is it bad for a man to be fat?
It is sad that Tom is mad.
Has Mum got the ham yet?
Is it fun to run in the wet?
The cat can sit on my lap, but that big dog cannot.
A cat is a pet and so is a dog, but a fox is not.
Is a rat a pet?

PROOF READING

What is wrong with these sentences?
**Ask the pupil to read them and put them right by filling in the
missing word or words:—**
My pen is my bag.
I got the pen the shop.
Bob Ben can get it.
Can Sam go us.
Sam left it the desk.
Len has got dog, he has not got cat.
Is empty?
Ben can get pen that shop.
Is Len his desk?

Fill in the *verbs* to make these into sentences
(reading only):—

Len _____ lunch at 2 o'clock.

Sam got home and _____ to bed.

Bob _____ wet in the rain.

We _____ to catch the bus.

Did you _____ the dog?

We _____ tea at 4 o'clock.

GAMES

Step game I

Using three phonetic words with which the pupil is familiar,
create a step.

   e.g. 'top' 'pet' 'tin'

Arrange them thus:—

```
              t   o   p
                      e
                      t   i   n
```

Now show this to the pupil, and set some for him to try.

Directional Game I

If the pupil has right/left confusion, ask him:—

   Show me your left eye.

   Show me your right leg.

   Show me your left hand.

Then progress to asking which is your own left and right eye
when you are facing the pupil — you may have to sit beside him
to begin with.

Memory Game

Teacher begins with "I went to the shops and I bought . . ."
(naming an object beginning with 'a').

Pupil repeats, "I went to the shops and I bought . . ." (he repeats
the teacher's object and adds one of his own beginning with 'b').

— 23 —

This continues with the list getting progressively longer and each new object has to begin with the next letter of the alphabet, until either teacher or pupil makes a mistake.

Consonant Blends

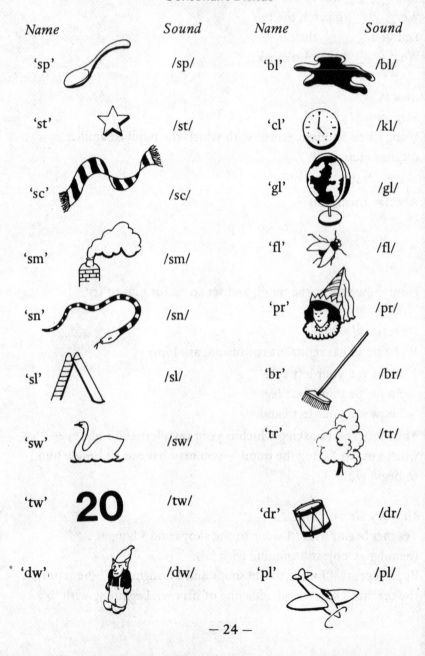

Name	Sound	Name	Sound
'sp'	/sp/	'bl'	/bl/
'st'	/st/	'cl'	/kl/
'sc'	/sc/	'gl'	/gl/
'sm'	/sm/	'fl'	/fl/
'sn'	/sn/	'pr'	/pr/
'sl'	/sl/	'br'	/br/
'sw'	/sw/	'tr'	/tr/
'tw'	/tw/	'dr'	/dr/
'dw'	/dw/	'pl'	/pl/

20

Name		Sound	Name		Sound
'cr'	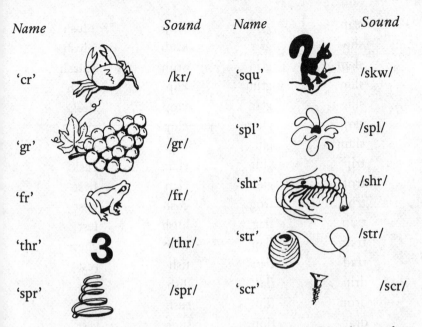	/kr/	'squ'		/skw/
'gr'		/gr/	'spl'		/spl/
'fr'		/fr/	'shr'		/shr/
'thr'	**3**	/thr/	'str'		/str/
'spr'		/spr/	'scr'		/scr/

Since much difficulty is encountered with these blends, much work will be needed on them.

It is suggested that they be taught as sound 'units' by the constant use of the consonant blend *Flashcards*. These will need to form a part of each lesson for some time to come, and even when apparently mastered will need occasional revision.

They should be taught both ways — that is, by presenting the card with the blend printed on it while the pupil says the sound, and writing the letters when the sound is said by the teacher.

Now You Can Make Many More Words

twig	drum	snip	much
twin	drug	snap	rich
spit	drag	plan	brush
spat	drab	plop	thrush
spin	grin	plot	flash
spot	Gran	plum	slosh
slit	grip	prop	crash
slot	grog	pram	crush

slap	grab	stop	blush
slip	grit	stub	plush
slam	grid	stun	splash
slim	grim	clip	slush
slug	glad	clop	desk
slop	glum	clog	risk
slum	glib	clap	tusk
trip	glut	clam	rusk
trot	glen	clan	best
trim	frog	cosh	nest
trap	flag	hush	lest
tram	flap	wish	chest
trad	flan	fish	rest
drip	flat	dish	test
drop	flip	rush	west
drat	flop	such	vest

ODD WORDS

when said

crest	held	soft	smut
quest	help	crisp	smog
request	self	lisp	snip
fist	himself	cloth	snap
mist	twelfth	froth	snag
twist	milk	adopt	snug
exist	silk	fret	snub
insist	left	Fred	from
cost	lift	Alf	bred
frost	loft	Alfred	prep
lost	belt	than	prop
bust	felt	that	prig
just	melt	them	prod
must	result	then	prim
rust	strut	thin	chin

trust	strap	him	shin
thrust	strip	Jim	chum
act	strum	rim	shun
fact	scrap	quit	chop
exact	scram	quid	shop
exactly	scrub	quip	shut
expect	film	equip	chug
respect	swim	brush	shift
next	swift	swish	chip
text	swam	flush	ship
flex	swig	mash	shod

SENTENCES FOR DICTATION (odd word — 'when')

Drop that crab, it bit me.

Alf has left his tin box in the loft.

I wish I did not have to sit at my desk.

It is such a fag to go to the shops when it is so hot.

I must rest, and go when it is not so hot.

The fish went flip flop on the slab.

I am glad I went on that trip to the U.S.A.

I am in such a rush to get to the flat.

Mum has got the ham and the plum flan, and Dad has got the grog, so we can have fun.

It is best to be slim and trim.

Tom got his gun and shot Fred in the chest.

Is the cash in the chest?

Pam has big hips; she is too fat.

Pam has a big bust.

I left my fish and chips at the shop.

Tom split six figs in bits.

Do not slip and drop the cup.

Alfred drops the cups with a crash.

The red flag is up, so we cannot swim.

Tom hit Ted with a cosh.

The flat is drab, but it is in a slum.

The sun sets in the west.

Can we go to the shed with Dad and help him fix the shelf?

As Gwen ran to the shed she cut her chin.

Drat that dog; he has left drips on the rug.

EXERCISES

Read these sentences and choose one of the words in the brackets to finish them, then *write* them out:—

Do not be so (grab, grog, glum, grin).

Jim dug up a (slop, slam, slim, slug).

To stun him he must be hit with a (cash, cosh, crush, mash).

We went on the (trim, trad, trip, tram).

We must run the (risk, rusk, desk, tusk).

I wish I had a bag of (crest, crust, crisps).

If it is left in the wet it will (just, rust, trust).

When it is red you must (stop, stub, stun).

It is a big drop from the top of the (flags, flats, flaps).

The film did not have much of a (plot, plop).

When do you get the results of the (exist, insist, exam)?

When she went for a swim fat Pam made a big (slush, splash, thrush).

We can go up in the (felt, left, lift).

"I must get (held, help)," he said.

N.B. Introduction of speech marks.

GAMES

Alphabet game II

Scatter alphabet letters on to the table, and ask the pupil to arrange them in order. If there is a mistake, cover the letters and ask the pupil to *recite* the alphabet. If he can do this correctly, uncover the letters and see if he can spot the mistake.

This game should be played regularly until the pupil can arrange the letters correctly in 1 min. 30 secs.

Step game II

Extend game I by asking the *pupil* to think of 'clues' for each step:—
'pet' — not a wild animal.
'top' — it spins.
'pin' — to hold things together.

Sound game

For pupils with difficulty in identifying letter sounds, play 'I spy'.
Play it first by giving the initial sound of the object to be guessed,
and later by giving the final sound of the object.
e.g. "I spy with my little eye something beginning with /b/ (object
— book), or something ending in /k/."

Directional game II

Extend game I by folding arms, crossing legs and then either wag
one finger and ask which hand it belongs to, or tap one foot and
ask which foot is tapping.

Hangman

Teacher and pupil take it in turns to think of a word (already in
his spelling vocabulary). The other one then guesses letters — if
they are correct they are entered in the word space, if not, a part
of the body is drawn until the man is complete, when he is hanged.

Lexicon

Play with the cards exposed on the table to enable you to see the
pupil's attempts at word making. Arrange the vowels in a row
above the consonants to emphasise that one of these must be used
to make every word.

Odd man out

Prepare a list of simple objects which fall into a recognisable category.
e.g. dog, cat, hen, fox, pig.
Ask the pupil which is the 'odd man'.
(Fox is 'odd' as it is wild as opposed to domestic.)
Set other, similar, tasks.

ASSIMILATION

Note for Teachers

There are only two letters that make their sounds down your nose — 'm' and 'n'. The first is made with your lips closed, and the second with your lips open.

Because we are lazy and it is easier to say 'jump' than 'junp', 'm' comes before 'p' or 'b' because they are all lip sounds, and 'n' comes before 't' 'd' or 'ch' because they are all tongue tip sounds.

Now, there is another nasal sound for which we do not have a symbol (or letter) and that is the /ng/ sound that comes before the back of tongue sounds /g/ and /k/. This sound is written as 'n', but it sounds like /ng/, once again because it is easier to say that way.

The voiced sounds /b/ and /g/ are not sounded in one-syllable words after 'm' and 'n':—

| thumb | lamb | sing | thing |

only in two-syllable words:—

| timber | jumbo | angry | finger |

These silent letter words and two-syllable words are only intended as examples. They are not to be given to the pupil to spell at this stage.

Now Try These Words
'n' before /t/ /d/ or /ch/ — 'm' before /p/

/a/	/e/	/i/	/o/	/u/
and	bend	wind	bond	fund
band	fend	flint	blond	blunt
brand	lend	hint	fond	grunt
grand	mend	lint	frond	hunt
hand	rend	mint	pond	shunt
land	send	stint	———	stunt
sand	spend	splint	stomp	bunch

/a/	/e/	/i/	/o/	/u/
stand	tend	tint	pomp	hunch
strand	bent	print	romp	lunch
grant*	lent	inch		munch
plant*	rent	finch		punch
branch*	sent	pinch		crunch
——	tent	winch		
camp	spent	——		clump
clamp	went	imp		dump
cramp	vent	limp		frump
damp	bench			hump
lamp	drench			jump
ramp	trench			lump
stamp	——			pump
tramp	empty			sump
vamp	attempt			stump
				trump

*the 'a' in these words tends to say /ar/

SENTENCES FOR DICTATION (odd words — 'you' 'friend')
When we mix the bran for the pig he grunts.
The band stand is in the big tent.
We trust you not to fish from that pond.
It is bad to hunt the fox.
I can stand on my hands.
The big blond man is a grand chap.
We went in the wet mud.
Meg stands by the bus stop with a hand up.
The wench had a gun in her hand.
Can you print this for me?
I can punch Jim on the chin.
Can we have ham for lunch?
Can we fish in that pond?
I am not fond of frogs.
I must be mad to spend so much cash.

I cannot stand this damp dump.

He just had a lump on his chin and a cut on his left hand.

I got a stamp from that shop.

Must you stamp so?

Stan has a limp; has he a bad leg?

Pam is such a frump.

Tom has the hump.

I got a lump when I bumped into the stump.

To camp is fun, but we must have a tent.

The man with a limp is a tramp.

I will be a <u>friend</u> to the <u>end</u>.

WORD SUMS

Word sums — that is, the adding of morphemes (either prefixes, suffixes or other words) to the root word to make new words:—

List I	*List II*
up + set = upset	ten + nis = tennis
up + on = upon	gob + let = goblet
in + to = into	bul + let = bullet
flag + ship = flagship	mag + net = magnet
grand + dad = grandad	trum + pet = trumpet
grand + ma = grandma	hus + band = husband
tal + cum = talcum	in + dex = index
hun + dred = hundred	prob + lem = problem
hum + bug = humbug	lim + pet = limpet
am + bush = ambush	rab + bit = rabbit

List III

be + yond = beyond	at + tend = attend
under + stand = understand	ex + tend = extend
de + fend = defend	de + pend = depend
in + tend = intend	ex + pand = expand
ex + tent = extent	con + tent = content

(These are only intended for older pupils, or at teacher's discretion.)

My husband cannot understand me.
We depend on him to help us get to the flagship.
I extend my hand to you, as a friend.
I must defend myself.
We must attend, or we bump into things.
"I am content with my lot," he said.
The pub is on the bend, beyond the pond.
This belt must expand or bust.
"I intend to go to a film," said Bob.
Tom defends Jim from Fred.
Grandma is not yet a hundred.
I do not intend to let you go.
The contents of that bag are on the shelf.
My husband is a humbug.
I had a problem with my trumpet.
"Get me a bag of humbugs from the shop," said Grandad.

EXERCISES: INTRODUCTION OF SPEECH MARKS
Read these sentences, choosing one of the words from the brackets
to complete them, then write them out:—
Tom can (jump, grump, stump) up the step.
I have (camp, cramp, clamp) in my left leg.
The milk is in the (goblet, limpet).
We crash into the stump with a (munch, lunch, crunch).
A sex-pot is a (tramp, vamp, trump).
My best pal is a (blend, bland, blond).
Run it up the (ramp, lamp, stamp).
I cannot (bend, lend, mend) you the cash.

GAMES
Alphabet game III
When the pupil has arranged the alphabet, tell him to turn away.
Remove all the vowels and close the gaps. Tell him to look at the
alphabet and ask him what you have done. See if he can replace
the vowels in their proper place.

Alphabet game IV
Recite the alphabet halting at 'j'. Ask the pupil to name the vowels
you have said so far. Now ask if he can name the others.

Step game III
Now make each step firmer:—

| 'sand' | 'dent' | 'tent' | 'sent' |

```
        s  a  n  d
        e        e
        n        n
        t  e  n  t
```

And Now These Words

/ng/

/ă/	/ĕ/	/ĭ/	/ŏ/	/ŭ/
bang	length	bring	gong	bung
clang	strength	cling	long	clung
fang		fling	along	dung
gang		ring	pong	flung
hang		sing	prong	hung
rang		sling	song	lung
sang		sting	strong	rung
sprang		string		stung
tang		spring		sprung
		swing		
		thing		
		wing		

/ngk/

bank	ink	rink	bonk	bunk
blank	blink	sink	clonk	clunk
crank	brink	shrink	honk	chunk
Frank	clink	stink	plonk	drunk

/ă/	/ĕ/	/ĭ/	/ŏ/	/ŭ/
prank	chink	think		funk
plank	drink	wink		hunk
rank	link	jinx		junk
sank	mink	minx		sunk
tank	pink	lynx		slunk
spank				shrunk
swank				trunk

ODD WORD
wrong

SENTENCES FOR DICTATION (odd word 'wrong') /ng/

I can swim a length.
Can you get me a length of string?
The blond man is strong.
Sing a song with me.
My hand is in a sling.
The dog sprang at me.
I flung myself at the swing and got on it.
This must be the wrong song.
"Hang that hag!" he said.
I go with that gang.
Bang went the gong.
Bring that thing to me.
Pam has a big red ring.
Chop up the long log.
The spring sprang up and hit me.
Did you ring Jim?
Fling it in the bin.
Hang it up on the peg.
The rat has big fangs.
Did you hang up the things?
The cat belongs to Tim.
Prod him with the prong.

We clung to the ship.
I can cling no longer.
This fish has a strong pong; it must be bad.
Do not slip the tip into the wrong hand!

SENTENCES FOR DICTATION /ngk/ and /ng/
I think that man is drunk.
I got that pink ink from the shop.
Can you bring Frank?
You must go to the bank to get the cash.
The river bank is sandy.
She has a big ring.
He went to the brink of the river.
Bring the wet rag to me.
I think we can get a drink at the club.
A ship has a gang plank.
She has a mink to swank.
Let's go to a Top Rank Bingo Club.
I rang Tom up.
She is a bit of a minx.
Do not spank him even if he is in the wrong.
Frank is fond of drink.
If you drink pink ink you shrink.
Drink up this hot milk.
I got this from the junk shop.
A junk can be a ship.
Can you wink?
Pam got shut in Grandad's trunk.
Clink, clunk, belt up.
I rank top in Maths.
"Thank you for the drink," my friend said.

Put these sentences into the past tense by adding 'ed' to the verb.

'ed' will never *sound* like /ed/. If it comes after a voiceless sound it will sound like a /t/ e.g. jumped; if after a voiced sound it will sound like a /d/ e.g. grabbed; or if after /t/ or /d/ it will sound like /id/.

The first sentence has been done for you: —
I rush with the wind.
I rushed with the wind.*

I land on the sand.
We camp on Ted's plot.*
I plant a pip in the pot.*
I bump into the stump.
We attempt to jump the gun.*
I mend his split pants.*
I limp into the pub.*
I jump into the pond.*

Now put the starred sentences into the present continuous by adding 'ing' to the verb and inserting the helper (or auxiliary) verb 'to be'.

    e.g. I am rushing with the wind.

GAMES
Parts in a whole I
Set out the word 'VEGETABLES' in large print. Divide a sheet of paper into two columns. Take turns and write one word each that can be found in the big word.

Vowel Consonant Digraph — 'ar'

car	harm	park	dart
bar	charm	shark	part
far	march	spark	smart

tar	ark	barn	start
scar	bark	darn	tart
star	dark	scarf	card
spar	hark	art	hard
arm	lark	cart	sharp
farm	mark	chart	Charles

ODD WORDS

half　　calf　　calm　　your　　are　　large

SENTENCES FOR DICTATION

It is dark in the loft.
Can you start your car?
A dart is sharp.
Is your bed hard or soft?
The car has no sparking plugs, so it cannot go.
Get in the cart and go to the farm.
It cannot do much harm if I have a lot of jam tarts.
She is so charming.
Are you going to get a charm for Pam?
It is just a lark.
Hark, hark, the lark; it must be spring.
Larks sing on the wing.
I got tar on my legs.
Can I have a star when I get top marks?
Is it far to march to the park?
"When can I start?" Dad said.
Charles is not a bad man; he just thinks he is.
Do not get your car from that car mart.
The dogs bark in the dark barn.
Park your car in the yard.
Mark has a long scarf.
Can you darn this for him?
Get the lard for Mum, then she can start on the tarts.
Send Dad a card.

A large part of this plum tart is bad.

Tom is top of the 'charts'.

March is the start of spring.

The cards are in the box.

Get yourself a jug of milk from the farm.

Has he cut his arm?

Dan is rich, he has six farms.

I am longing to get a star on my chart.

This pump is hard. Will you help me?

In the park is a swing. It hit Gwen on the leg and cut it.

If it is calm we can go and swim.

"Half a calf is too large to bring from the shop in my car," said
    Charles.

WORD SUMS

tar + get = target	dar + ling = darling
arm + y = army	part + ly = partly
hard + ly = hardly	part + y = party
gar + den = garden	de + part = depart
re + gard = regard	car + pet = carpet
a + larm = alarm	sharp + ly = sharply
mar + ket = market	smart + ly = smartly

SENTENCES FOR WORD SUMS (older pupils only)

This pig went to market.

The bus departs at six.

In the army you must be smart.

She raps him smartly on the hand.

The alarm went at six, so I had to get up.

We have a big garden.

That shot was hardly on target; it went left of the mark.

Gwen went to a party.

It is partly wrong.

The carpet is a bit thin.

You are my darling.

I must sharpen this thing. It must be sharpened.

He sent his regards.

Fill in the missing parts of these word sums:—

Did you hit the tar . . .?

Join the arm . and be smart.

The dog wet the car . . .

We went to shop in the mar . . .

I re . . . . you with . larm when you bang the top of your desk.

I must go and dig the gar . . .

We can hard . . go yet.

The part . must end at ten.

Unscramble these sentences (the first has been done for you):—

In the car you can park your yard.

You can park your car in the yard.

Fangs big sharks have.

Darts go and pubs together.

Go to the must you with the dogs park.

You cows fields find in.

GAMES

Alphabet game V

Divide the letters between teacher and pupil. At a given signal each holds a letter under the table. The pupil is asked to name the letter he is holding, then to place it on the table. He is told the name of the teacher's letter then he can be asked to recite the alphabet from one of the letters to the next, or to say what other letter comes before or after one or other letter. This can be expanded later so that he holds a letter in each hand and must name them sequentially without looking at them.

Direction game III
Teach the points of the compass, and explain how to use an atlas, with north at the top and south at the bottom.

Step game IV
This now becomes a crossword. The pupil drafts this by first filling in the words, and then thinking of the clues.

SAMPLE CROSSWORD

CLUES

Across

1. Remove 'm' from 'many'.
3. I can spin.
6. Opposite of 'down'.
8. Opposite of 'yes'.
10. Come .. lunch.
11. Same as 8 across, but add a 't'.

Down

1. Take 'n' from 'Ann'.
2. Haven't you finished . . .?
4. . . . it down!
5. Opposite of 'out'.
7. Another name for 'Dad'.
9. Opposite of 'under'.

1. Tom and Pam went to the park with the dogs, Rex and Gus.
   Rex is a big dog, but Gus is not so big. Rex barks, but Gus yaps.
   Rex and Gus have fun with a cat and it jumps on a stump and
   spits at them. At six Tom, Pam, Rex and Gus must go, as
   it is dark.

2. Fred stops his car and slips into the bank. With his gun on his
   hip he yells "Up with your hands"! The man at the desk lets
   Fred get the cash and he then dashes to the car and is lost in the
   dark and fog.

ANAGRAMS ('ar' words) 'jumbled words'

SARTS   — they shine at night = stars
DARGEN — where flowers grow =
KARTEM — where you can buy cheap things =
CHMAR   — it brings good luck =
TARCH   — I mark your progress on it =
FARSC   — to put round your neck =

Vowel Consonant Digraphs

'or'	'er'
or	her
for	herd
born	shepherd
corn	fern
morn	stern
torn	tern
form	herb
storm	verb
port	nerve*
sort	serve*
short	verse*
sport	berth

— 42 —

'*o͡r*'	'*e͡r*'
sn<u>or</u>t	sist<u>er</u>
f<u>or</u>k	silv<u>er</u>
st<u>or</u>k	s<u>er</u>vant
c<u>or</u>d	exp<u>er</u>t
l<u>or</u>d	c<u>er</u>tain*
f<u>or</u>th	
n<u>or</u>th	
c<u>or</u>ner	
h<u>or</u>se*	

ODD WORDS

were   very   every

*reading only at this stage; introduce for spelling on p. 87 and p. 84.

Note that 'er' is an unusual spelling in the middle of words, but at the end it is the most common spelling of all.

  e.g.   lett<u>er</u>   moth<u>er</u>   fath<u>er</u>   butt<u>er</u>
or comparatives, e.g. shorter, sharper, longer;
and introduce superlative 'est', e.g. shortest, sharpest, longest.

SENTENCES FOR DICTATION ('or' words):—
Fred gets up in the morning.
I am top of the form.
The ship is in port.
Sam is very short and fat.
Sam is a sport, even if he is fat and short.
You can dig the garden with a fork.
The wind is from the north.
Alf is very grand; he is a lord.
Do not stand on the farmer's corn.
Let us go forth and storm the fort.
A chart is a sort of map.
My pants cannot be torn.
A pig snorts, but a dog barks.

A stork has long legs.
Sport is fun, but hunting is not fun for the fox.
Stand in the corner.

It is dark in the mornings when it is winter.
She left her hat in the car.
The herbs are in the larder.
Is 'sing' a verb?
Is 'song' a verb?
Go and stand in the corner.
It is the end of term.
The shepherd lost his job.
Ted is a stern man.
The herd is in the pen.

WORD SUMS

form + er = former

per + form = perform

re + port = report

ex + port = export

car + port = carport

or + der = order

north + ern = northern

ac + cord = accord

tend + er = tender

per + son = person

per + mit = permit

in + form = inform

plat + form = platform

re + port + er = reporter

de + port = deport

re + cord = record

bor + der = border

for + ty = forty

accord + ing = according

fend + er = fender

per + haps = perhaps

per + fect = perfect

(These are only for older pupils, but they are all AA and A words.)

SENTENCES FOR DICTATION (word sums)
I bent the bumper on the car.
A bumper is a sort of fender.
Pam had a bad report, but Jim is top of the form.
The Northern border is over-run.

I must inform you that you are a bad performer.
He can export cars if he has a permit.
According to this we can order forty cans.
He is a shifty person.
Perhaps you will permit me to inform them that we do not wish
   to go.
I got a thorn in my finger.

ODD WORDS

	sword	snore	horde	
more	before	shore	store	bore
core	score	tore	wore	swore

SENTENCES FOR DICTATION (odd words)
This sword is blunt.
Hordes of men storm the fort with swords.
I must have more for lunch than just buns.
Jim has the top score.
We went to the store to get the order.
The core of this plum is bad.
I wore my best pants and tore them.
Let us go by car to the shore.
This is such a bore.
I tore my best pants before I wore them.
That's torn it!
He swore at me when I trod on him.
Can I store this in the corner of the shed?

GAMES
Treasure Island
Draw an imaginary island. Pupil marks places with directional
names — 'South Farm', 'North Inlet' — clues are given for him to
find the 'treasure' by turning in the right direction.

'treasure' = sweets   'pace' = 1 cm.

THE 'W' RULE

'W' is a very powerful letter. He is a sort of Wizard who can Wave his Wand and change himself into a vowel (as we shall see later), make himself invisible (as in wrong), or perhaps one should say 'soundless', make other letters silent (as in when), and even change the sounds of some letters that come after him.

RULE I

'a' after 'w' saying /ŏ/

(Words given with their frequency 'word count', so only teach AA and A words to the younger or less able pupil.)

was AA	wasp 13	swab 1
want AA	wand 12	swat 1
what AA	wad 2	watch * AA
wash AA	swamp 29	Washington * A
whatever AA	swan 19	swallow * 48
wander A	swap 2	warrant * 20

*reading only at this stage.

ODD WORD

water

SHORT FORMS

wasn't = was not   it's = it is

(Introduction of apostrophe for missing letters)

SENTENCES FOR DICTATION

It was hot.

What do you want?

I want a wash.

Do not wander so far from the camp.

It wasn't much fun at the party.

I swim in the water.

I wash my hands in the water.
You must not splash the water.
"What a lot of swans on the water," said Jim.
I wasn't stung by the wasp.
He had a wad of cash.
I want to swap my stamps.
The bad man sank in the swamp.
She had a wand with a star on top.
Whatever came over him?
Swat that wasp.
A swab was left in him.

'a' after 'qu' saying /ŏ/

Because 'qu' says /kw/ the /w/ sound has the same effect on an 'a'
coming after 'qu' as it does when it comes after 'w'.

| quad 1 | squat 6 | squadron * 10 |
| squad 6 | squash 6 | squabble * 2 |

(These are not very high count words, so only give them if it is
thought appropriate.)
*reading only at this stage.

SENTENCES FOR DICTATION ('a' after 'qu')
Tesco let you have quad stamps.
Pam had quads. Wasn't she clever?
Squat on this log.
Do you want a drink of squash?
That squad is smart.

EXERCISES
Turn these statements into questions.
(The first has been done for you.)
The wind is strong.
Is the wind strong?
The sand is soft.

The tent has split.
The gong is ringing.
Ringo was singing.
Tom is shut in the shed.
I must go to bed.
A wasp can sting.

Fill in 'want' or 'what' and copy the sentences.

_____ I _____ for Christmas is a gun.

_____ do you _____ to do with it?

_____ did she say?

I don't _____ it.

_____ is the good of all this work?

_____ a smashing party it was.

I _____ to wander in the park in the dark.

THE 'W' RULE

RULE II

'ar' after 'w' saying /or/

war AA	towards 44	ward 18
warm AA	reward 43	wharf 12
warn A	dwarf 25	warp 12
toward AA	swarm 22	swarthy 4
	quart 17	quarter AA

(The last two are included because 'qu' says /kw/, remember?)

WORD SUM

war + ship = warship

SENTENCES FOR DICTATION

I warned you not to go to the wharf.
You are to get a reward.
It is so warm, I want a long drink.

That is a swarm of wasps.
Go toward the farm and it's on your left.
He ran towards me.
Get a quart of milk at the shop.
A quarter of a plum tart is not much.
The warship hit the target.

ODD WORDS

forward AA   upward 32   backward 27

(The stress is on the first syllable in these words, so the last syllable has a 'shwa' sound to it /wəd/.)

I cannot get this car to go forward.
We must go upward towards the top.

WIZZOFF THE WIZARD OF THE WORLD OF WORDS

RULE III

'or' after 'w' saying /er/

word AA	worth AA	worse * A
work AA	worthy A	worm 37
world AA	worship A	worthless 15

SENTENCES FOR DICTATION
This is hard work.
That is not the word I want.
The world is very big.
A rich man is worth a lot.
I wish you did not worship such a lot of pop stars.
It is just a bit of worthless junk.
He is not worthy of her.
The worst thing in the world is work.
You are a worm.
You must stand up for yourself.

You dig up worms in the garden.
War work was worthy.

poor   door   floor   moor

SENTENCES FOR DICTATION
Poor Pam sat on the floor.
It is windy up on the moor.
Open the door.
Shut the door.
The floor is wet.

EXERCISES

SHORT FORMS

Mr. = Mister (first and last letter used).
Mrs. = Mistress (first, middle and last letter used — pronounced 'missis').
Dr. = Doctor (first and last letter used).

SENTENCES FOR DICTATION
Dr. Smith can rush to the ward if he is wanted.
Mrs. Peg can go to the party, but Mr. Peg has to work.
Dr. Bland is a worthy man; he works hard.
Mr. Bond is worthless; he never works.
Mrs. Prendy wants a map of the world.

SHORT FORMS

can't = cannot   won't = will not

SENTENCES FOR DICTATION
Mrs. Stamp won't be going to the shops yet.
I can't do this work; it is so hard.
Mrs. Swank can't put on her mink, as it is in store.

Stand   stand up,   stand by,   stand in.

Think of sentences to use them.
Now think of different meanings for 'lift' and 'punch'.

'll'

One syllable words ending in /l/ which have a *short* vowel take
double 'll':—

/ă/	/ĕ/	/ĭ/	/ŏ/	/ŭ/
all	bell	ill	doll	dull
ball	fell	bill	roll*	gull
call	hell	fill		hull
fall	sell	frill		bull*
hall	shell	grill		pull*
small	smell	hill		full*
stall	spell	mill		
tall	swell	pill		
wall	tell	shrill		
shall*	well	spill		
	yell	still		
		thrill		
		till		
		will		

*Note that 'shall' is the only word that has its proper short /ă/
sound and the 'u' in bull, pull and full sounds like /o͝o/. You will
find that 'o' and 'u' are very good friends and often sound like
one another.

SENTENCES FOR DICTATION ('ll')
Shall I call them in?
I rang the door bell.
Can you pull me up?

I must spell well, so I will work hard.
That shrill yell will send me mad.
I got a thrill by the wishing well.
Send the bill for the pills to Bill.
Mrs. Bull is on the pill.
Top up your car with Shell before you go on the M1.
This is dull work, but spelling is a must.
Tom won't want a doll, nor will he want this bill.
If you fall from that tall wall you will end up in a ward.
"I can pull you up this hill," said Bob to his friend.
This small shell has a bad smell.
What shall I tell her?
You will be quids in if you can sell that rusty car for £50.
Can we trust him, or will he do us?

SHORT FORM

don't = do not.

SENTENCES

Don't fall in the water if you can't swim.
I won't do it if you don't want me to.
Can't you tell that I don't want you to go?
I still don't want to work.

MINUS WORD SUMS

— taking bits off to get to 'root word'.
   e.g. establishmentarianism
Can you show the steps to get to the root word 'stable'?

WORD SUMS

be + fell = befell
in + stall = install
re + fill = refill
up + hill = uphill

re + sell = resell
un + well = unwell
un + till = until*
hall + mark = hallmark

*Note loss of one 'l'.

Fill in 'they' or 'there' and copy the sentences.

_____ went _____ with Bill.

Did _____ say that the man went _ ___?

_____ _____ are after all!

_____ all went _____ in Bill's car.

Can _____ park _____?

The men are _____.

_____ are not _____ yet.

_____ we are; it's all over.

SHORT FORMS

I'm	= I am	I'll	= I will
he's	= he is	he'll	= he will
she's	= she is	she'll	= she will
you're	= you are	you'll	= you will
we're	= we are	we'll	= we will
they're	= they are	they'll	= they will

ODD WORDS

they   who

Who do they think they are?

Are they all coming to the film?

EXERCISES

Replace these with their 'short forms'. (The first has been done for you.)

I am not well.

I'm not well.

He is top of the list.

She is too fat.

He is a bad lot.

We are all going with you.

They are all in the hall.

You will not be going to the party.

You are the best person in the form.
Do not do that.
I cannot do it.
I will not do it.

Now expand these.
I'm so fed up.
He's drunk, I think.
We're not very well.
You're a pig.
They'll never win.

Scale these down (possessive pronouns).
(The first has been done for you.)
The trunk belongs to Bill.
It belongs to him.
It is his.
The hat belongs to Jim.
The bag belongs to Mum.

'a' before 'l' saying /aw/

talk AA	salt AA	false A
walk AA	halt 29	Walter 25
chalk A	alter 10	scald 9
stalk 27	malt 6	bald 8

ODD WORD

fault A

Give AA words only to younger pupils, or those who find this difficult.

SENTENCES FOR DICTATION
Must you talk so much?

Let us go for a walk.
Brush the chalk from your hands.
Cut this stalk with something sharp.
Let me have the salt.
When it is red you must come to a halt.
The poor man is bald.
Hot water will scald your hands.
Come for a drink at the 'Bull and Bush'.
Push the door; don't pull it.

come	some	put
become	something	bush
		push

Note once again how the 'o' and 'u' have changed places with one another. The 'o' sounding like /ŭ/ and the 'u' like /o͝o/.

EXERCISES

ONE WORD – LOTS OF MEANINGS

(Read these sentences.)
Flowers have green stalks.
A lion stalks its prey.
He stalked out of the room.
Sherlock Holmes wore a deer stalker hat.
but
A <u>stork</u> is a bird with wings.

Put these into the negative and use short forms.
(The first has been done for you.)
He can come for a walk.
He can't come for a walk.
Jim is the best walker in my form.
This is the longest scarf in the world.
Pam was the worst at sport.

I can go to the ball.
Sam and Pam will be going at six.

Turn these back into the affirmative.
(Some words need changing.)
I have spent all my cash.
Dad did not lend the car to Ben. (lent)
Mum has not lost her mink.
Len did not run over the dog. (ran)
I can't be at Bob's by ten.
I won't be going to the party. (will)
I don't think that remark upset her.

'ss'

One syllable words ending in /s/ or /z/ which have a *short* vowel,
and no other letter (consonant) before the last sound, take double
'ss' or 'zz':—

/ă/	/ĕ/	/ĭ/	/ŏ/	/ŭ/
ass	Bess	hiss	boss	fuss
lass	chess	miss	cross	buzz
mass	dress	Miss	floss	fuzz
jazz	less	Swiss	gloss	
brass*	mess	fizz	loss	
class*	press	whizz	moss	
glass*	stress		toss	
grass*	guess			
pass*				

Note that the 'a' in these words (southern English) has an /ar/
sound.

EXCEPTIONS TO DOUBLE 'ss'

(but these are known already)

is   his   has   yes   this   thus   us   gas   bus

These are all lexical items, except gas and bus which are abbreviations.

ODD WORDS

puss   pussy

Once again the 'u' in 'puss' has the same /ŏŏ/ sound as in 'put'.

SENTENCES FOR DICTATION ('ss')

Mr. and Mrs. Smith are cross.

The Swiss miss has lost her pussy.

Put that mess under the bush.

I am in a mess.

I want cress sandwiches for lunch.

Lord Sandwich invented the sandwich.

Bess has torn her pink dress.

A cross boss will win the toss.

Fussy Lizzy is in a tizzy.

The 'fuzz' got him as he went for his gun.

Don't harm the swan or it'll hiss at you.

I got top marks and passed the test.

This drink is fizzy.

I am dizzy.

Miss Smith sat on a hot cross bun. She squashed it flat, so she was
    cross as well.

Press my dress for me, Bess.

Len and Pam will get the bus if they rush.

I am best at chess.

Spit will put a gloss on it.

Can we cross at this spot?

The door bell went buzz.

We can sit on the grass.

My class is best this term.

We must go the party for the boss.

He can't stand his boss.

I passed the blond man at the bus stop.

Read these sentences, choose a word from the brackets to finish them, then write them out.

I am in a (chess, mess, less).

She is good at (mess, less, chess).

My dress wants a (Bess, mess, press).

He left the mess on the floor, so she made a (buzz, fuzz, fuss).

He is a silly (lass, mass, ass).

She won the (boss, toss, loss).

Fill in the missing word. ('ss' words)

I want a _____ of water.

I have more than Pam, so she has _____ than me.

_____ me the salt.

The door knob is _____.

Bess is a big plump _____ lass.

I want some candy _____.

We go to _____ in the morning.

'Well' as a prefix loses one 'l' e.g. welcome, welfare

So does 'all' e.g. also, altogether

We welcome you to the party.

I also want a glass of water.

We are ten altogether.

GAMES

Parts in a whole II

How many little words in TELEVISION?

Make it a timed activity now.

One letter — many sounds

After giving the sentences, ask the pupil to underline, in different colours, the different sounds of the letter 'a'.

  e.g. 'Pass the salt Pam'. In this sentence 'a' says /ar/, /or/ and /ă/.

Alphabet game VI
Divide letters as before, but now ask all sorts of questions about
the letters put in the centre of the table.
1. Which letter comes first?
2. What letter comes after this?
3. What letter comes before this?
4. Recite the alphabet from the first letter to the second.
5. How many vowels have you said?

Other alphabet games
'Alphabet dominoes' using 'M' as central first letter, each in
turn placing letters in their correct position from those in central
pile, or after sharing out 13 letters each.

    Asking pupil to pick up and give name of letter before/after
one specified by teacher.

104 WORDS IN TELEVISION

one	tile	vent	stein
in	teens	violent	stone
invite	toil	viol	sieve
oil	tine	vies	seel
evil	toes	levi	stele
elite	tiles	lesion	slit
isle	tins	lest	slot
inlet	tone	list	sloe
inset	tinsel	live	solve
ions	toils	lion	solvent
insole	tens	loin	sole
into	tonsil	lent	stole
even	to	lien	stile
evens	eel	lint	silent
olive	eve	love	sten
onset	event	lost	site
oils	vision	listen	sleet
enlist	vein	lies	seven

elves	velt	lions	senile
envies	vest	lens	sloven
oven	vine	loins	Noel
vet	vile	lone	note
nest	nose	liven	novel
noes	noise	steel	nit
silo	soil	silt	lees
veil	veto	lee	seen

Look up the unfamiliar words in the dictionary.

'a' before 's' saying /ar/

Here are some more words where the 'a' before 's' sounds like /ar/:—

ask AA	task A	plaster 16
fast AA	castle* A	rascal* 12
last AA	fasten 40	ghastly* 10
past AA	blast 31	nasty 7
master AA	clasp 27	grasp 36
cast A	mast 26	flask 4
vast A	mask 17	bask 3
basket A		

*reading only at this stage.
(Once again only give AA and A words to those who find it difficult.)

Pupils will have grasped the idea that you can add morphemes, 'prefixes and suffixes', to root words by now, because of all the word sums we have been doing. From now on, then, we will add them to the words on the spelling list, and not give them as separate word sum exercises.

ODD WORDS

purr   egg   odd   add   too

Mr. Marks has a fast car.

Tom wants a faster car too.

You have come at last.

It is past ten.

We went past the spot.

All that is in the past.

I did not win. In fact, I was last.

We are the last to get on the bus.

Run fast for the last bus.

I have run past the stop.

The blast shot the door in, and hit Mark in the chest.

Blast it! I have spelled it wrong.

To bask in the sun is fun.

Do not put all your eggs in this basket.

To spell is a hard task.

He is a hard task master.

Fill this flask with hot milk.

That is a nasty cut; put some plaster on it.

Fasten this trunk for me.

Can you add? I am very bad at it.

Clasp my hand when we cross.

Can you grasp it? Do you understand?

Grasp the ring and pull.

What an odd word 'ghastly' is.

'Purr' is an odd word too. A dog barks, but a cat purrs.

We wore masks at the ball.

A tall ship has a mast.

The world is vast; it is very big.

'ff'

One syllable words ending in /f/ with a *short* vowel, take double 'ff':—

/ă/	/ĭ/	/ŏ/	/ŭ/
staff*	cliff	off	bluff
chaff*	sniff	doff	cuff
	stiff	toff	huff
	tiff		muff
			puff
			snuff
			stuff

Exceptions:— if, of.

*Note once again that 'a' before 'f' tends to sound like /ar/. 'Off' always comes *after* a verb, which is present or understood.

    e.g. jump off, 'off' to school.

Here are some more words with 'a' saying /ar/:—

after AA	shaft 25	raft 7
afterwards 47	craft 21	daft 1

(Only give the AA word 'after' to youngsters.)

'a' before 'th' saying /ar/

Because /f/ and /th/ are so alike, 'a' sometimes says /ar/ before 'th':—

path AA	father AA
bath 46	rather AA

ODD WORDS

England   English   pretty

SENTENCES FOR DICTATION
This is the staff car park.
Cliff is a smart chap.

He pushed her off the cliff.
I get all my stuff from Marks and Sparks.
Tom must get off the hard stuff.
I huff and I puff when I go up the hill.
I am not bluffing.
I had a tiff with my husband.
We must starch it to get it stiff.
This stuff is too stiff.
We are short of staff.
Run a bath for your father.
Don't be daft! this isn't the cliff path!
She is a pretty English miss.
England is pretty in the spring.
Put your hands in my muff to warm them.

READING AND WRITING FOR MEANING
Fill in 'of' or 'off' or 'for'.
She fell ____ the top ____ the flats.
We must be ____, it's half past ten.
We went on top ____ the bus ____ a bit.
You must take ____ your pants before you jump into bed ____
   the night.
Get ____ your bike and get me a bag ____ crisps from that shop.
   I want them ____ tea.
I have a lot ____ sums to do ____ prep.
The alarm went ____ at six. ____ once it woke me up.

'ck'

One syllable words ending in /k/ with a *short* vowel and no other
letter (consonant) before the last /k/ sound take 'ck'. They cannot
take double 'kk' like the others we have been doing, because we
do not get double 'kk' in English.

/ă/	/ĕ/	/ĭ/	/ŏ/	/ŭ/
back	beck	brick	block	buck
black	deck	crick	cock	bucket
clack	fleck	cricket	clock	chuck
crack	neck	chick	dock	cluck
hack	peck	chicken	flock	duck
Jack	speck	Dick	frock	luck
jacket		lick	Jock	muck
lack		pick	lock	puck
mack		prick	locket	pluck
mackintosh		quick	rock	ruck
pack		sick	rocket	suck
quack		sicken	shock	stuck
rack		spick	sock	struck
racket		thick	stock	shuck
sack		tick	stocking	tuck
tack		ticket	pock	truck
attack		wick	pocket	
track		wicket		
tracking				

Teacher's note

Refer back to page 10 for suffixes.

ODD WORDS

knob   knit   knock   trek   wreck   wrist   wren

gnat   any   many   anything   wrap

o'clock

('o' is short for 'of the', so 'of the clock')

Note that if there is a silent letter before an 'n' it will be 'k' or 'g' and if there is a silent letter before a 'r' it will be a 'w'.

SENTENCES FOR DICTATION

The dust is thick on this shelf.

Fat Jack has got the sack.

Dick has a sack on his back.

Stick up your hands; this is a hijack.

Can you do this card trick?

You will get the sack if you rob the till.

Dick has got very thin after starting to slim.

Even a fork truck can't lift this lot.

Mr. Jack Ash is back in harness.

We got a shock when the car hit the wall.

We went to a shocking film.

I will be back by six o'clock.

The cat has sicked it up on the carpet.

Gwen gets sick in a car; isn't it sickening?

I have a crick in my neck.

Cricket was started by the English.

It's not cricket to trick your pals.

Jack went in to bat on a sticky wicket.

The ball knocked off his stumps.

We shall want a rucksack to trek in the hills.

Remember that you never start a word with 'ck'.

EXERCISES

Fill in 'c', 'k', or 'ck' in the following words: —

This must be the wrong tra___, it is just a mud path.

Can you go to the ban_ for me and get the cash?

I do want a drin_ of water.

Ja___ put the sa___ on his ba___ and went off with the stuff.

I want a boo_ to loo_ at.

The thug gave Fred a _rack on the ba___ of the ne___ with a thi___ sti___.

_luck, _luck went the hen as we fed her.

I have a han_y in my po___et.

We ran qui___ly when the ro___et went off.

The gnat bit me.

Can you knit this for me?

It is a brass knob.

"Undo this knot", said Pat to Jack.

My wrist is in plaster.

Wrap it up for Grandma.

Add 'ed' 'ing' or 'et' to these 'ck' words so that the sentence makes sense:—

The ship will be dock____ at ten o'clock.

I was shock____ by that nasty remark.

Bill pick____ the man's pock____ and got a wad of cash.

This is a lock____ for your neck.

The bad man was lock____ up.

Do not kick the buck____ just yet!

Just my luck to be track____ the wrong chap!

The ducks are quack____ on the pond; they want to be fed.

That is a nasty mark on your jack____ Jock.

That pin is prick____ me.

Jack and Pat are neck____ in the back of the car.

We all flock____ to the shock____ film.

You will get fat after tuck____ in to so much grub.

The poor chicken is pluck____ for the lunch.

What we are lack____ is a stock of thick stock____.

The boss sack____ Bill for not going to work.

This cup is crack____.

What a crack____ batsman Jack is.

I wonder if we will send a rock____ to Mars?

Get me a tick____ to go on the bus.

DICTATED STORY

Jack and Nick went to the park with Rex, the dog, and a big red ball. They lost the ball under a black truck, so Jack ran back to tell his Mum. Nick and Rex went on and met Dick. They had lots of fun on the swings and things and forgot Rex. Rex ran off and got lost. Mum had asked them to be back by dark and it was dark at six o'clock, but they are not back yet. When Dick did get back he got a smack from his Mum. Nick was not so lucky, he got a hard spanking from Dad. Then Rex was at the door, yelping, so they let him in and all was well at last.

Answer these questions.
Who went to the park?
What did they take with them?
What did they do at the park?
Did they get back before dark?
What happened when they got back?

Choose a word to complete the sentence.
This pretty (rocket, socket, locket) will go well with her pink dress.
We must get a (picket, cricket, ticket) to go on the bus.
A small chicken is a (chick, pick, sick).

GAMES
Parts in a whole III
How many words in 'CATASTROPHE'?
How many words in 'AEROPLANE'?

Now put the first ten in alphabetical order.

Short forms game

Expand these:—	*Shorten these:—*
isn't	he had
wasn't	they had
can't	he is
won't	does not
it's	cannot
let's	will not

This is an appropriate place to teach *Rule I of Endings* (page 000) to those pupils who might benefit. It follows quite logically upon the previous section dealing with doubled consonants.

Anagrams (words with double letter endings)

LELB	– it rings
FLICF	– a man's name
SLAGS	– to drink from
TRUCKS	– he _____ her with his fist
KCUD	– swims on water

LONG VOWELS

Teacher's notes

So far we have been using only the five short vowels:–

ă   ĕ   ĭ   ŏ   ŭ

the three vowel/cŏnsonant digraphs:–

ar   or   er

and 'open syllable' long vowels in words like:–

mē   hē   shē   wē   bȳ   mȳ   gō   sō   nō

An 'open syllable' is one that ends in a vowel, as in the words above.

A closed syllable ends in a consonant, and then the vowel is always *short*:–

ăt   răn   bĕd   fĕd   ĭll   ĭt   ŏff   ŭp

We are now going to do *magic or lengthening 'e'* which is really a re-opening of the syllable as you add the 'e' after the final consonant and this makes the vowel *long* (or say its name).

VOWEL – CONSONANT – E

V – C – E

ā	ăt	āte
me	mĕt	mēte
bȳ	bĭt	bīte
nō	nŏt	nōte

a — e

	List I		List II
ăt	āte	băr	bāre
hăt	hāte	căr	cāre
făt	fāte	făr	fāre
măt	māte	măr	māre
răt	rāte	scăr	scāre
măd	māde	stăr	stāre
Săm	sāme	lăck	lāke
căn	cāne	măck	māke
măn	māne	răck	rake
păn	pāne	stăck	stāke
căp	cāpe	ăll	āle
năp	nāpe	băll	bāle
scrăp	scrape	stăll	stale
tăp	tāpe	tăll	tāle
Căm	cāme	băth	bāthe

Teacher's note

Give only List I if List II is too difficult. In any case give only
one list at a time. Notice the loss of the final double letter when
the vowel goes long. Not in the case of 'bathe' because 'th' is a
digraph. Notice also that words ending in 'ar' sound like /āer/
when the vowel goes long. It is of academic interest to note that
the 'th' becomes voiced when the vowel is long.

The Cam is a river in England. He fell in the Cam.

He came at me full tilt.

It was at the ball that I lost my bag.

She ate till she was sick.

It is my fate to be fat.

I don't think that hat is for you, I hate it.

You're on the mat, mate.

We won't get rid of the rats at this rate.

It was the din that made him mad.

Sam is in the same class as me.

The master can hit him with the cane.

The man pats the horse's mane.

She flung the pan at the glass door and splintered a pane.

He put on his cap and cape.

Stop the water from that tap with a bit of sticky tape.

I had a scrap with that chap and got into a scrape.

We can get a drink at the bar.

You must cover your bare arms.

Wash your car with care.

That cut on her leg will mar the mare.

I want a nap.

Jack struck him on the nape of his neck.

Is it far to Westminster?

What is the fare?

He has a nasty cut on his arm, will it scar?

You don't scare me.

I got ten stars for this work.

Don't stare at me.

Make him bring a mack.

Put your hat on the rack, then get a rake from the garden shed.

We all want ale to drink.

That is your ball.

Put these into bales.

We sat in the stalls.

This cake is <u>stale</u>.

He is very <u>tall</u> and strong.

That was a short <u>tale</u> to tell.

Get in the <u>bath</u> and have a wash.

We will all <u>bathe</u> in the water in the summer.

Choose a word from the brackets:—

He wants (fame, tame, shame).

He came for a (lake, wake, game) all the same.

You are late for the (quake, date, fate) that we made.

Shut the (mate, late, gate).

Put this in the (snake, safe, shake).

Have you sent Dad to the (maze, craze, laze)? He will get lost.

e — e

Teacher's note

A very unusual spelling in one syllable words. Not very usual in polysyllabic ones either.

e.g.   athlete   complete   extreme   recede

We can only think of three examples of one syllable words, and they are not very good:—

met	mete
her	here
the	these

ODD WORDS

there   were   where

SENTENCES FOR DICTATION

Where are my things?

Over there.

Here are your things.
Where can I put these?
I met her here.
Where were you going?
Were you going with her?
We were all going to go to the maze at Hampton.
What were you going to the shops for?
What were you doing when I came in?
Where is it?
Where is what?

EXERCISES
Make these statements into questions using the 'helper verb'
(auxiliary) 'to do'.
(The first one has been done for you.)
You think he is a brave man.
<u>Do</u> you think he is a brave man?
She had a good shape.
He had to park there.
We went for a ride in the car.
Sam picks up his chicken in his fingers.
I care when you make mistakes.

Now turn these questions back into statements.
Did you make these stale cakes?
Do you care what you put on in the morning?
Does your father shave every day?
Does Dick tell bad jokes?
Did you put these things over here?
Does she tell you where she is going?

ANAGRAMS (a — words)
MABEL   — what you get when you do something wrong.
VERAB   — a person who is not afraid
HAVES   — a man must do it every morning

— 72 —

MALE — what you are when you have a limp
SLACES — what you get on in the morning to see if you are too fat

i — e

List I		*List II*	
pip	pipe	grim	grime
rip	ripe	slim	slime
pin	pine	till	tile
fin	fine	still	stile
din	dine	fill	file
win	wine	lick	like
spin	spine	quit	quite
bit	bite	sir	sire
spit	spite	fir	fire
rid	ride	trip	tripe
slid	slide	strip	stripe

Teacher's note

Once again List I is easier than List II, so do the same as with a — e.
Note once more the loss of doubling when the vowel goes long,
and the /er/ sound in words ending in 'r'.

ODD WORDS

white   while   knife   write   style

SENTENCES FOR DICTATION
Sit here while I write this for you.
This grape has lots of pips.
Don't rip your pants, I have just mended them.
This plum isn't ripe.
Do not quit, even if it is quite long.
I must just pin up this hem.
He won't pine for long.
There are a lot of pines in Switzerland.

A fish has <u>fins</u>; just <u>fine</u> for fish.

There is such a <u>din</u> when we <u>dine</u> with the children.

I must <u>win</u> with this ticket, the prize is some fine <u>wine</u>.

<u>Spin</u> a fine tale for them.

Your <u>spine</u> runs up your back.

She is rather <u>thin</u>.

"<u>Thine</u> is the Kingdom."

I wish I were <u>slim</u>.

He slid in the <u>slime</u>.

The <u>fir</u> tree is on <u>fire</u>.

Mick <u>slid</u> in the mud.

We can <u>slide</u> here, the mud is thicker.

Get <u>rid</u> of her and we'll go for a <u>ride</u>.

The dog <u>bit</u> me on the leg — a big, bad <u>bite</u>.

I want to <u>trip</u> him up.

I hate <u>tripe</u>.

The cash is in the <u>till</u>.

The <u>tile</u> fell off in the wind.

Are you <u>still</u> here?

Jump off the <u>stile</u>.

"<u>Fill</u> her up to the top," he said.

Have you got a <u>file</u>?

You can have a <u>lick</u> of this ice if you <u>like</u>.

<u>Sir</u>, what is a <u>sire</u>?

o — e

List I		List II	
cŏd	cōde	slŏp	slōpe
cŏp	cōpe	rŏt	rōte
hŏp	hōpe	tŏt	tōte
mŏp	mōpe	clŏth	clōthe
nŏt	nōte	dŏll	dōle
pŏp	pōpe	smŏck	smōke
rŏd	rōde	cŏck	cōke
rŏb	rōbe	blŏck	blōke

Give only List I to younger pupils, and note once more the loss of doubling when the vowel goes long, and the voicing of the 'th' in 'clothe'.

SENTENCES FOR DICTATION

Cod is not a fish I care for.

This is in code; I don't understand it.

You will cop it when you get back.

I can't cope with these sums.

Hop as far as you can, and I will time you.

I hope you can come.

Mop up that mess.

Don't mope, he'll be back.

This is not her note.

I'd like a drink of pop.

The Pope is the father of the Church of Rome.

The rod for the fishing line is in the back of the car.

We rode all along by the river on those rusty bikes.

I won't rob you.

Look in the wardrobe.

Don't slop the water all over the floor.

Don't be a dope! You'll slip on that slope!

What a lot of rot.

This is a rote task.

Pam is just a tot.

We can win a lot on the tote.

Get me a cloth to mop this up.

Hang your clothes up when you take them off.

Jane has a talking doll.

He is on the dole poor man; he can't get work.

The farmer wore a smock.

You can smoke if you like.

The cock is a male chicken.

I want a drink of coke.

wrote　　four　　pour　　tour　　gnome

The four of us can go on this tour.
Will you pour me out four cups of water.
I wrote to Mum four times while on tour.

u — e

List I		List II	
cŭb	cūbe	plŭm	plūme
tŭb	tūbe	ŭs	ūse
mŭt	mūte	fŭss	fūse
cŭt	cūte	lŭck	Lūke
shŭt	chūte	pŭrr	pūre

Teacher's note

Use your discretion as to which words to give, and note again the loss of doubling when the vowel goes long, and the voicing of the 's' in 'fuse' and 'use'.

SENTENCES FOR DICTATION

The fox had six <u>cubs</u>.
A <u>cube</u> is square like this block.
Plants in <u>tubs</u> must have lots of water.
We came by <u>tube</u> this morning.
<u>Shut</u> up! I want to work.
We have a <u>chute</u> for the waste.
I hate <u>plums</u>.
Charles had a <u>plume</u> in his hat.
Don't <u>fuss</u>! It's just a <u>fuse</u>.
<u>Luke</u> has such <u>luck</u>!
The cat will <u>purr</u> if you stroke her.
Is that water <u>pure</u>?

do   does   done   go   goes   gone
who   whose   whom   whole   during

SENTENCES FOR DICTATION   (odd words)

Have you <u>done</u> your homework?

<u>Does</u> it upset you if I smoke?

Has she <u>gone</u> yet?

She <u>goes</u> on and on, nag nag nag.

The <u>whole</u> thing was a bad joke.

I have a <u>hole</u> in this sock.

<u>Who</u> are you?

<u>Whose</u> cat is that?

To <u>whom</u> does it belong?

It was <u>during</u> the film that I lost my handbag. Do you think somebody stole it?

ODD WORDS

sure   sugar

SENTENCES FOR DICTATION

Are you <u>sure</u> you do not want to come?

I am <u>sure</u> to slip up on that slope.

It is <u>sure</u> to be wet if I have my best dress on.

Get me some <u>sugar</u>, will you?

Do you want some <u>sugar</u> on your cornflakes?

<u>Sugar</u> is bad for you if you want to slim.

Are you <u>sure</u> you don't want <u>sugar</u>?

This <u>sugar</u> has <u>gone</u> lumpy.

If you make jam, lump <u>sugar</u> is best.

This <u>whole</u> cake is <u>sure</u> to make me sick.

Other Lazy 'e' Words for Practice

came	arrive	hose	June
became	drive	nose	rude
cake	crime	pose	crude
cave	dive	rose	exclude
base	five	doze	prude
case	life	froze	tune
brave	line	bone	prune
date	mile	home	include
game	mine	close	flute
gate	bride	lone	lute
escape	glide	alone	excuse
fare	hide	chose	refuse
fame	hire	those	recluse
gave	acquire	suppose	rule
make	inquire	broke	acute
name	require	broken	mute
safe	smile	spoke	shute
shape	nine	spoken	cube
shave	side	joke	tube
square	tide	hole	nude
stale	wide	hove	fortune
quake	time	grove	pure
snake	prize	stove	cure
gaze	size	strode	picture
laze	rise	cove	nature
maze	wise	clove	future
eve	wire	drove	adventure

See pages 158-9 for longer words if needed.

Story Writing

Now that all the 'wh' question words have been taught, it is possible to make a start on creative writing.

Using the following skeleton plan, a sensible, coherent story can be told by the pupil and then written down firstly by the teacher (at the pupil's direction) then by the pupil.

The story must answer these questions:—

1. *Who* did it?
2. *Where* did it happen?
3. *When* did it happen?
4. *What* happened?
5. *Why* did it happen?
6. *Which* way did it end?

If the story answers these six questions it *is* a 'good' story. Tell the pupil that these are the only words beginning with 'wh' that they need to know at this stage.

This will form the basis for later exercises in creative writing.

N.B. Spelling and punctuation must be somewhat disregarded in creative writing at first.

EXERCISES: LANGUAGE USAGE

Turn these STATEMENTS into QUESTIONS by adding a 'tag'.
(The first two have been done for you.)

He chose that rose.
He chose that rose, didn't he?
You mustn't pose like that
You mustn't pose like that, must you?
We got lost in the maze.
Tom has a big nose.
My cake won't rise.
He is a wise man.
It's just a bit of wasteland.
We didn't bathe in the lake.
It was fun on the slide.
I'm not sickening for 'flu.

He is a wise man.
It's just a bit of wasteland.
We didn't bathe in the lake.
It was fun on the slide.
I'm not sickening for 'flu.
You haven't woken her up.
Golf is a craze with him.
A wave of crime has hit England.
Wales isn't my homeland.
You will choke if you drink so fast.
He didn't get the prize.
You can't help me with this lot.

Teacher's note

Add an affirmative 'tag' to a negative statement, and a negative 'tag' to an affirmative statement. This is a suitable place to teach *Rule II of Endings* (see page 142) to those pupils who might benefit.

THE 'V' RULE

No English word ends in 'v'; there is always an 'e' after it. That is why 'have' has an 'e' on the end although the 'a' is short.
Live and līve are both spelled the same way for the same reason:—
We live at home
That is a live wire.
Also there is no such spelling as 'uv', so all words with an /ŭv/ sound in them are spelled with an 'o'. After all, if it isn't a 'u', what other letter can it be but 'u's very good friend 'o'?

love　　dove　　oven　　above
glove　　cover　　discover

ODD WORDS

mother　　brother　　grandmother
other　　another

— 80 —

I've	I have
you've	you have
we've	we have
they've	they have

SENTENCES FOR DICTATION

Give me five pegs for the washing line.

He picked up her glove and gave her a hug.

I love you, darling.

I love my mother.

Alfred gave Robert a shove.

Put the cover on and pop it in the oven.

The dove must take cover, or it will be shot.

Doves live in dove-cotes.

Who can discover where the dog has his bone?

My mother has a brother and a sister.

Jack has another brother, called Tom.

Have you any brothers and sisters?

My grandmother lives in Devon.

My other grandmother lives in Bexhill.

Poor Tom hasn't got a mother or a father.

This valve won't close.

I must serve well to win from Pat.

She had a nerve to sing that rude verse.

EXERCISE

Replace the subject with a 'wh' word pronoun, turning the statement into a question:—

Jane made the beds. (Who made the beds?)

The dog bit him.

Charles wants a turn on the slide.

My book got torn.

The slide belongs to me. (whose)

More Words with 'o' Saying /ŭ/

Once again 'o' and 'u' are being good friends and changing places:—

none	nothing	among	amongst
month	monk	front	income
sometimes	London	Monday*	dozen*
wonder	money*	honey*	sponge*
monkey*	son	ton	won
accomplish*			

ODD WORDS

one   once   only

tongue   roll

SENTENCES FOR DICTATION

Moses was in a basket amongst the bulrushes.

Jim was among those who escaped.

It's among the tins on the top shelf.

It must be amongst that junk somewhere.

This is the shortest month of all.

In what month were you born?

I live in London. Where do you live?

We must put some more plaster on the front wall.

As you are the smallest you must stand in front.

Dick is in the front of the class, Jack is at the back.

Once upon a time there was a gib bad wolf.

EXERCISES

Put these sentences into the NEGATIVE and then into NEGATIVE QUESTIONS (the first has been done for you):—

Frank has a big income.

Frank does not have a big income. (negative)

Doesn't Frank have a big income? (negative question)

Jack wants to be a monk.
Fred likes living in London.
Pat wants to go in the front of the plane.
Her mother was on the stage.
Her father is worth a lot of money.
Dr. Jones is a quick worker.
Mrs. Jones is even quicker.

ANTONYMS AND SYNONYMS

LANGUAGE USAGE

We have met HOMONYMS — words which sound the same but
have different meanings (and sometimes slightly different spelling)
— now we meet:—

ANTONYMS — words of opposite meaning.
SYNONYMS — different words with the same meaning.

The ANTONYM of 'front' is 'back'.
A SYNONYM for 'front' is 'fore'.

The opposite of 'moon' is (sun, nun, bun).
Monkey is the same as (cape, shape, ape).
The opposite of nothing is (sometime, somewhere, something).
Sire is the same as (mother, father, brother).

HARD AND SOFT SOUNDS

Soft 'c' — 'c' saying /s/

You remember that at the beginning of this programme you were
told that 'c' said /k/, the same as 'k', and that all words began with
a 'c' and ended with a 'k'? Well, now you are going to find out
that sometimes 'c' says /s/, and this is when the next letter is:—

e   i   y

There are not many words *beginning* with *soft 'c'* and they are nearly all long, difficult words, so we are giving you a list of the most common ones which are for *reading only*:—

cent AA	cell A
centre AA	cease A
circle AA	civil A
city AA	citizen A
certain AA	circumstance A
certainly AA	central A
century	circus
cycle	

SENTENCES FOR READING
I spent my last cent on drink.
We live in the centre of the city.
You can make a circle with a pair of compasses.
Are you certain you can go? Certainly I am.
He scored a 100 runs at cricket; that is a century.
Put this thug in a prison cell.
All work will cease if the factory shuts.
He was not very civil to me. In fact, he was rather rude.
You must do your duty as a citizen.
Certainly we are civilized (civilised).
There is civil war in Ulster.
Piccadilly Circus is not on the Central Line.
Western civilisation will not last long if all this strife does not cease.
Can you cycle to the park to see the cygnets?

Soft 'c' in the middle of words
This is much more usual, but again they are rather long, difficult words. Still, remember that 'ce' and 'ci' are more common than 'se' and 'si' *in the middle of words*:—

except AA	recent A	pencil 41
accept AA	recently A	conceal 39
decide AA	concern A	magnificent 37
success AA	council A	incident 29
necessary AA	excite 47	concert 21
December A	medicine 46	sincere 20
accident A	innocent 41	decent 18
	parcel 23	

FLASHCARD GAME ON SOFT AND HARD 'C'
Available in *Alpha to Omega Flashcards*.

SENTENCES FOR DICTATION
We can all accept your invitation, except Peter.
When did you decide to study medicine?
The accident was last December.
He is an innocent man; don't send him to prison.
To be su*cce*ssful you need two collars and three socks, but only
    one collar and two socks are really ne*ce*ssary.
His concern for you is sincere.
The concert was magnificent.
Lend me your pencil, I've broken mine.
I don't think that dress is decent.
Try not to excite the dog or he will bark.
The incident is closed; don't speak of it again.
My God! Your husband! I must conceal myself in the wardrobe.

SENTENCES FOR DICTATION   (older pupils)
When did you decide to come home?
It was a wet December.
We had a nasty accident.
We came up to London to tour the city.
I am very hard up; I haven't a cent.
The cell was small and dark.
Mexico is in the centre of a cyclone.

Soft 'c' at the end of words

This is the most usual spelling of all. In fact, if you hear a /s/ sound at the end of a word which has a *long* vowel it is much more likely to be spelt 'ce' than 'se'.

List I		List II	
ace	ice	advance	pence
face	dice	dance	fence
grace	lice	chance	absence
lace	mice	France	difference
pace	nice	glance	service
place	price	romance	office
race	rice	instance	justice
space	spice	distance	police
trace	trice	stance	notice
puce	slice	circumstance	since
	twice	palace	Prince
		entrance	force
			sentence

Teacher's note

Since this is the most usual spelling for the sound /s/ at word end, in particular after long vowels, it is here that the pupil's attention should be focused at first.

SENTENCES FOR DICTATION

This is a nice place, but not a nice price.

Do you want some ice in your drink?

I don't like mice, even as pets.

Did you bake this nice cake, Grace?

Her lace glove is on the floor; that's all.

Tom went puce in the face when Grace was rude to him.

Hang on! I'll be there in a trice.

It was a nice romance, even if it didn't last long.

I met her at a dance last spring.
I got these tickets for France in advance.
Cinderella met her Prince at a dance.
I have not had a date since Grace went to France.
Can I be of service? Yes, can you lend me five pence?
The police put up that notice in the office.
I am fed up with my boss, so I have given my notice.

EXCEPTIONS (with 'se' finally)

base	case	chase	dose
horse	false	else	tense
expense	sense	nonsense	house*
mouse*	loose*	noose	promise*

*reading only at this stage.

SENTENCES FOR DICTATION
The case with the broken clasp is mine.
In that case I will go back to base one.
What else can you do besides ride a horse?
Shall I ask someone else what the dose is?
To tell me that his name is false is just nonsense.

Words beginning with 'K'

You will now see why some words begin with a 'k', because if they began with a 'c' the first sound would be /s/ and not /k/:—

List I		List II ('sk')
keg	kilo*	Eskimo
Ken	kind*	skid
ketchup*	king	skiff
key	kipper*	skill
kick	kiss	skim

kid	kit	skin
kidnap	kite	skip
kill	kitchen*	skimp
kilt	keel*	sketch*
keen*	keep*	skirt*
kennel*	kerchief*	skeleton*
kettle*	kidney*	skittle*

*reading only at this stage.

SENTENCES FOR DICTATION

Ken has a keg of rum.

I'd rather have a kiss than a kick.

We gave the kid a kit to make a kite.

The King will kidnap the kid and kill him.

The Scotsman wore a kilt.

The sun will take the skin off your nose.

Eskimos rub noses, but don't kiss or shake hands.

EXCEPTIONS ('k' used with 'a' or 'u')

skate   skull (This word can be spelt 'scull' but then it means
         something different.)

The lake is frozen, so we can skate.

She skims over the ice on her skates.

What do these expressions really mean?

To skate on thin ice.

To skate over something.

Skull

He fell off his bike but did not crack his skull.

He has a hard skull.   (What is the difference in meaning

He has a thick skull.   in those two sentences?)

You <u>scull</u> on the water.

Fill in 'k' 'c' or 'ck' in the blanks:—

_ut a sli_e of c_k_ for Gra_e.

She can dan_e with gra_e and charm.

His name is _en.

A _ind man will not _ill you.

He is not that _ind of man.

If I s_ip lunch I will have time to go to the shops.

Bla__ is the opposite of white.

Soft 'g'

'g' saying /j/

Like 'c' 'g' *usually* says /j/ when the next letter is:—

e	i	y

Soft 'g' is not so common at the *beginning* of words, but is *always* used in the *middle* or at the *end* of words.

Soft 'g' at the beginning of words

George	AA	giant	A	gem	24
German	AA	gently	46	Egypt	22
gentle*	AA	generous*	40	ginger	13
gentleman*	AA	genius*	30	gypsy	9
general	AA	gesture	28	gin	4

*reading only at this stage.

EXCEPTIONS

get AA   girl AA   give AA   begin AA   gift A

Teacher's note

Unlike soft 'c' which has virtually no exceptions (even 'sceptical' is sometimes spelt 'skeptical'), soft 'g' has a number of exceptions. We have only given the high count ones.

George fell into the gorge and broke his neck.

The German giant gently lifted the gypsy into a gem of a car and
  gave her some gin.

Soft 'g' in the middle of words

danger*	AA	energy	41	tragedy*	27
suggest*	AA	register	41	intelligent*	27
engine*	A	engineer*	40	legend	22
digest	A	agent	40	regiment	21
imagine*	A	magic*	39	emergency	19
stranger*	A	pigeon*	34	pageant*	11
angel*	47	agency	32	algebra	3

*reading only at this stage.

SENTENCES FOR READING

George, you are in danger from the stranger.

Ginger is a giant of a man.

The German is an agent for Egypt.

The red engine had gone to London.

I imagine you won't want any more cake after that huge lunch.

Here is the gin; help yourself.

The gypsy will tell your fortune.

George likes ginger cake.

The emergency exit is over there.

It was a tragedy that the intelligent girl did not pass her algebra
  exam.

The regiment marched past in full dress uniform.

She was a legend in her lifetime.

We are going to the magic circle.

This is the best agency in the city.

Soft 'g' at the end of words

	List I		List II	
	age	binge	college*	AA
	cage	mingy	passage*	AA
	page	singe	village*	AA
	rage	tinge	manage*	A
	stage	sponge	average*	A
	wage	plunge	savage*	40
	engage	charge	damage*	32
	change	discharge	image*	31
	exchange	recharge	revenge*	29
	cringe	large	refuge*	21
	fringe	enlarge	cabbage*	16
	hinge	barge	garage*	14
	forge	bulge	bandage*	14
	gorge	indulge	baggage*	11
	huge	bilge	postage*	10

*reading only at this stage, or for spelling if the teacher feels the pupil can manage it, in which case the word counts have been given.

MNEMONIC RHYME

No English word can end in 'j'
This is a rule you <u>must</u> obey.

SENTENCES FOR DICTATION

A stag has fine antlers.
Do not let her go on the stage Mrs. Worthington.
This is a rag of a dress.
Father is in a rage.
Did the agency engage you for the part of Peter Pan in the pantomime?
Pam and George are on the verge of an engagement.
Don't wag your finger at me!
Can you live well on your wage?
She has had that fringe for some time.
Take the plunge! The water is not all that bad.

What do you charge for a wash and set?

This dress is too large; I will give it to Pam. She is huge!

Take care he does not lunge at you with that sharp sword.

Do you indulge in strong drink?

We all went on a barge tour up the river Avon.

All went well till George fell in.

You must be brave and not cringe when you go to the dentist.

ODD WORDS

soldier   orange   enemy

The regiment charged the enemy.

Soldiers wage war.

He is my worst enemy.

Soldiers have to be brave.

There is a legend that the soldiers charged over there towards the hill.

FLASHCARD GAME ON HARD AND SOFT 'G'

LIST II WORDS IN SENTENCES FOR DICTATION

FOR MORE ADVANCED PUPILS

If I can pass this exam I want to go to college.

Poor Tom is the village idiot.

Can you manage to reverse the car into the garage?

I lost all my baggage going to France.

I must get a large white cabbage.

The postage has gone up again.

Mrs. Smith backed into the lamp post and did a lot of damage to the car.

The average man cannot manage to fill in an Income Tax Form.

The back passage was blocked with garbage.

Do you know what these overworked similies really mean?

Pale as a ghost

Black as thunder

Mad as a hatter

Hot as Hell
Cold as ice
Thick as two planks
Clear as mud
Bold as brass
Bald as a coot

Can you think of any more?

FLASHCARD GAME I — Write a hard, or a soft 'c' word in 20 blank playing cards (10 of each). Use as a sorting, pairs or snap game. Or use games in *Alpha to Omega Flashcards*.

FLASHCARD GAME II — ditto with hard and soft 'g' words.

PROOF READING
What is wrong with these sentences?
Read them first, then see if you can spell them correctly:—
Was Gohn a good cing?
Excimos live on ike.
This cace is stale.
Do you lice kider?
This larg orang is for you.
You are the imij of Gim.
Call the polise.
I want to be a soljer when I am big.
The caj is too small for this big kat.
Klumsy Klot, you have dropped the lot!
Krumbs, what a mess!
Let's gog trot to the park.
The guj sent him to gug.
Don't get cross, it was only a goke.
Give me a ciss, Bess.
The car went into a scid and skared me stiff.
The Skotsman's cilt went up in the wind, and he had no pants
    under it!
I have lost my cey, and cannot open the door.

— 93 —

Words Beginning With 'J'

You will now see why some words begin with 'j' — it is when the next letter is an '<u>a</u>' '<u>o</u>' '<u>u</u>' :—

jab	jazz	James	Jock	
Jack	jot	Jane	judge*	AA
jacket	jog	Janet	July*	A
jam	jug	John	January*	A
job	joke	June	jolly*	22
jump	just	jar	jockey*	2

*reading only at this stage.

EXCEPTIONS

Jill   jet

SENTENCES FOR DICTATION

Jack and Jill went up the hill.

He got a jet plane to France.

Jane has a necklace of jet.

Janet and John drop a jar of jam on James for a joke.

Jack's jacket is too hot for June.

June does not care a jot, she has another job to do.

Jock will jog in Regent's Park before lunch.

EXERCISES

How many ways can you use the word 'hand'?

What is the ANTONYM of 'small'?

Give a SYNONYM for 'small'.

WALLS

'u' as a 'wall' to stop 'g' going soft in such words as:—

guess	guest	guide	guilt	guy
vague	plague	vogue	rogue	

Guess what he has in his hand.

John was my guest for lunch.

Be my guest.

James will guide us on the tour of France.

Jane has a guide dog.

Guy is a soldier in the army.

We put a guy on the bonfire on the fifth of November.

Do you think she is the guilty party?

He is rather vague; he never tells us what he does.

The plague of London was at its worst in 1665.

Must you plague me with all this work?

Long dresses are all the vogue.

He is a rogue, he not only pinched my bum but all my money.

A rogue is someone who has left the herd.

Note paper is non-U; it is the vogue to call it writing paper.

The guide in Switzerland was a smashing guy.

I wish to confess my guilt.

'd' as a wall to keep the vowel *short* in words such as:—

/ă/	/ĕ/	/ĭ/	/ŏ/	/ŭ/
badge	edge	bridge	lodge	budge
badger	hedge	midge	lodger	budget
cadge	ledge	midget	podge	fudge
Madge	ledger	ridge	splodge	judge
	sledge		stodge	nudge
	dredge		dodge	trudge
	wedge			sludge
				smudge
				grudge

SENTENCES FOR DICTATION

Don't sit on the edge; you'll fall in.

The bridge across the river has gone.

Give him a nudge to wake him up.

That man in a wig is a judge.

I must trudge home alone, I suppose.

I have overspent my budget.

Make these present continuous by adding 'ing' to the verb, adding the helper verb 'to be':—

The podgy lodger ate all my fudge. (is eating)

Madge will cadge some more from that midget.

I made this stodgy cake.

We went to Cambridge for a short while.

I will wedge the door with this.

The blazing plane went over the ridge.

I made a budget and stuck to it.

Dad plants the hedge to stop the badgers.

't' as a Wall for No Reason at All!

'tch'

(only happens in words with a *short* vowel)

/ă/	/ĕ/	/ĭ/	/ŏ/	/ŭ/
batch	fetch	itch	Scotch	Dutch
catch	ketch	bitch		hutch
hatch	ketchup	ditch		clutch
hatchet	sketch	kitchen		butch
latch	stretch	pitch		butcher
match	wretch	stitch		
patch		witch		
scratch		bewitch		
snatch		switch		
watch				

SENTENCES FOR DICTATION

The witch waved her wand and made the Prince into a frog.

I bet you can't catch me.

Put the catch on the door so it won't close.

Catch the ball and pass it on.

Can you let me have a match?

I must watch this cricket match.

I am no match for her.

If you have an itch, scratch it!

He is a scratch golfer.

EXCEPTIONS

such   much   rich   which

(but these are already known)

WORDS WITH A LONG VOWEL SOUND
BUT A SHORT VOWEL SPELLING

bīnd	wīnd	bōld	tōld
blīnd	pīnt	cōld	hōst
grīnd	chīld	fōld	mōst
fīnd	mīld	enfōld	almōst
hīnd	wīld	gōld	pōst
behīnd	bōlt	golden	ghōst
kīnd	cōlt	hōld	bōth
mīnd	jōlt	sōld	yōlk
rīnd	ōld	scōld	fōlk

SENTENCES FOR DICTATION

Mind that poor old man, he is blind.

Jack jumped at me from behind the door and gave me a shock.

Alice opened the garden door with a golden key.

I cannot ride that wild colt, it will bolt with me.

Drink a pint of milk a day.

Do you mind if I get off here and fetch the liver from the butcher?

Did you catch the last post?

Mr. James Bender got a golden handshake when he left his job.

One pint of milk will not stretch that far.

Hold my hand when we cross at the crossing.
You simply must catch up on your work or you will be all behind.

ODD WORDS

clīmb bŏmb lămb tōmb

sign signal signature design resign

SENTENCES FOR DICTATION
Give me a sign.
Will you sign here?
Do you mind signing twice?
Is that your signature?
I met a ghost on the landing.
It was the ghost of my mother.
She gave me a sign to come with her.
It was very ghostly!
There was a ghostly signature on the wall.

SHORT PASSAGE OF DICTATION WITH 'ODD WORDS'
Once upon a time there was a chap called John. His <u>mother</u> sent
him to fetch <u>some</u> <u>water</u>. Poor John picked up the <u>wrong</u> bucket,
<u>which</u> had a hole in it. <u>While</u> he was <u>walk</u>ing back it left drips on
the <u>floor</u>. When he came to the <u>door</u> he <u>push</u>ed it open, but the
wet <u>floor</u> made him slip. What a <u>wreck</u> — <u>water</u> every<u>where</u>!
<u>Before</u> he can mop it up his mother <u>come</u>s home. "What have
<u>you</u> <u>done</u>?" she snorts, "Your <u>father</u> will have to <u>talk</u> to you
<u>when</u> he gets home". But John <u>doesn't</u> care, he goes off on a
<u>tour</u> and <u>only</u> <u>comes</u> back <u>when</u> the <u>whole</u> thing is forgotten.

How many short forms can you remember?

Spelling Test to be Given at End of Stage I

sad	ten	pin	bun	on
jut	pot	beg	big	fox
from	split	crash	rich	help
scrub	splash	thrush	pinch	plug
when	thing	think	went	go
scarf	form	serve	more	before
was	squash	war	forward	work
poor	ball	pull	they	who
talk	come	class	last	add
off	bath	half	pretty	England
sock	any	hate	bathe	like
there	were	quite	while	write
smoke	four	use	does	during
sure	oven	mother	none	only
twice	chance	else	skid	skate
get	age	sponge	soldier	orange
joke	guess	edge	dodge	smudge
snatch	watch	kind	ghost	sign

Marking note for teachers

Less than 45 correct — Stage I not truly mastered. Note all errors — revise — re-administer.

45-55 . . . . Fair (should re-test later)
56-69 . . . . Good
Over 70 . . . . Excellent

Stage II

Now we come to the other ways of spelling long vowels in one syllable words. In these words two vowels (or a vowel and a semi-vowel) are put together to give the *long* vowel sound.

Remember that:—

When two vowels go out walking
The *first* vowel does the talking

So, in each case, the sound that you *hear* will be the *first* letter of each pair.

Each of these long vowels has two different spellings; one being used medially (in the middle of words) and the other finally (at the end of words).

The exception to this pattern is tiresome 'e' again which, although it, too, has two possible spellings, 'ee' and 'ea' both can be used either medially or finally.

Long /ā/ has 'ai' medially and 'ay' finally.
Long /ō/ has 'oa' medially and 'ow' finally.
Long /ī/ has 'igh' medially and 'y' finally.
Long /ū/ has 'oo' medially and 'ew' finally.
Long /ē/ has 'ee' and 'ea' both medially and finally.

Long /a/

Medially 'ai'	Finally 'ay'	Medially 'ai'	Finally 'ay'
brain	day	fail	stray
drain	today	nail	astray

Medially 'ai'	Finally 'ay'	Medially 'ai'	Finally 'ay'
pain	may	pail	pray
rain	dismay	rail	spray
train	say	sail	sway
Spain	pay	tail	railway
plain	repay	aim	holiday
explain	bay	claim	okay
stain	lay	exclaim	
strain	delay	air	
gain	ray	chair	
again	way	fair	
against	away	unfair	
await	always	affair	
main	play	hair	
remain	display	pair	
aid	tray	repair	
maid	betray	despair	
paid	clay	stair	
afraid	gay	praise	
wait	hay	raise	
await	stay	maintain	

ODD WORDS

Britain   straight   their   obey   two

SENTENCES FOR DICTATION

I have such a ghastly pain I think I must be ill.

Is it still raining?

Can you explain all this to me?

The strain is too much for me.

Mr. Stan Smith was told to restrain his dog.

I can hardly restrain myself when that man with the blond wig
comes on the box.

"Stand up against the wall with your hands up", <u>said</u> the larger of the <u>two</u> thugs.

Mind where you dig, the main drain runs there.

"Have you paid the maid?," asked Jane.

I can't go on waiting for you for ever, you must make up your mind.

You haven't gone and spilt the paint again, have you?

Aim straight for the centre of the target.

I am in despair over all this work.

Are you certain they went there?

The smell of this paint will make me faint.

The train came in on time today.

There was a disaster when the train ran off the railway line.

Did she say she wants more pay? Send her away.

Charles has gone upstairs with the tray.

Are you going to Spain for your holiday, or will you have to stay in <u>Britain</u>?

Go and play somewhere else.

We went on the dodgems at the fair.

No one loves a fairy when she's old!

EXERCISES

**Choose one of the words in the brackets,
then write out the sentence (homophones).**

There is cold water in that (pale, pail).

Her face went (pale, pail) when she met him.

That is a fairy (tale, tail).

I hope to get a bargain at the (sale, sail).

We had to put up another (sale, sail) to catch what wind there was.

James has a (pane, pain) in his neck, poor man.

You can stroke the (mane, main) of a horse.

Do we go on the (mane, main) line to Waterloo?

I (made, maid) a nasty stain on my best dress.

Fill in 'their' or 'there'.

Is that _____ house over _____?

This is _____ dog, isn't it?

Where did you put it, here or _____?

John and Peter got _____ coats from the wardrobe and put them on.

Stay _____ and don't move!

Teacher's note

If 'ai' is reversed it splits into two syllables and the first vowel is long.

   e.g. di/al tri/al di/amond di/agram di/ary Di/ana

Fill in the missing words.
(They all have a long /a/ sound, but some are spelt 'ai' and some 'a – e'.)

Jim had such a bad _____ we had to send for Dr. Jones.

He gave him some pills to _____.

You wash the floor, but you _____ the rugs.

You must _____ your way to that landmark.

_____ until the ice is thick before you _____ on it.

Jane was in a rush as she was _____ for her date.

Come to the _____ and we'll go on the dodgems.

THE POSSESSIVE APOSTROPHE

(used to show ownership)

e.g. Jane's hat = the hat belongs to Jane.

Now try working these out:–
   Mark's scarf.
   Jim's jumper.
   Janet's crossword.

Now the other way — what do these become?

The dog belongs to Pat.

The cape belongs to Len.

The car belongs to Mr. Ashcroft.

The garden belongs to Mrs. Smith.

The game belongs to the boys.

The house belongs to the man.

Long /ō/

Medially 'oa'	*Finally* 'ow'
oat	bow
boat	elbow
coat	blow
float	crow
goat	flow
throat	glow
load	grow
road	know
toad	low
coal	below
foal	mow
goal	row
loaf	slow
moan	show
groan	snow
Joan	stow
loan	
oak	*Rule breakers*
soak	own
soap	bowl
oath	grown

We now meet 'w' being a vowel, and remember that it is the *first* vowel that gives you the vowel sound. If you reverse 'oa' it splits into two syllables, the first vowel being long.

e.g. chā/os

SENTENCES FOR DICTATION
This boat will not float, it has a hole in it.
I want a thicker coat for the winter.
John got hold of the goat by the throat when it kicked him.
Will you take this load of coal upstairs for Dr. Redman?
This road is very bumpy, I wonder where it goes? Nowhere, I
    suspect.
He shot a splendid goal just before time.
Get me a sliced loaf from Mr. Johnson's shop.
He loafs all day doing nothing.
Joan moans and groans when she has to work.
You will have to have a lot of soap and a long soak in the bath to
    get off all that mud.
The black crow makes a nest with twigs.
I know you are here, it's your car in the drive.
You must mow the grass, it's up to my chest.
This is a very slow train, the slowest train of the day.
This chair is much too low.
Lower the boats, the ship is going to sink.
Whose flat is below this one?

EXCEPTIONS TO 'OW' AT THE END OF WORDS
toe   foe   hoe   Joe

SENTENCES FOR DICTATION
George let forth an oath when I trod on his toe.
We have ten fingers and ten toes.
An ape's toes are just like fingers.
The Germans were the foe in World War I.

They were the foe in World War II as well!
Go and hoe the garden, James, it is a mess.
Joe let Joan have a loan to get herself a car.
It was only a small car, but it cost a lot!

ODD WORDS

brooch   though   although   shoe   canoe   cocoa

SENTENCES FOR DICTATION

If we both stow away the Captain will be sure to know.
I can only find one shoe, which is not much use.
A canoe is fun if you can swim, and don't mind being wet and
   cold.
Although I am small I am very strong.
Hot cocoa makes a nice drink at bedtime.
Jane is good at Maths, though her sister is not.
These shoes are very smart but they pinch.

Teacher's note

If 'oe' appears within a word it splits into two separate syllables.

e.g.   pō/em   cō/ercion

Long /ū/

Teacher's note

This pattern is not as straightforward as long /ā/ and long /ō/,
since the letter 'ū' only appears in a few words. Also there are
three sounds — /u/ /o͞o/ and /o͝o/. The double 'oo' spelling is not
so surprising as 'o' and 'u' are such good friends, but 'ew' is more
difficult to understand. It comes from Old English, while 'ue'
comes from the German.

| Medially | | Finally | |
'oo'		'ew'	
fo͞od	mo͞od	new	/ū/
ho͞of	co͞ol	few	/ū/
fo͞ol	po͞ol	dew	/ū/
scho͞ol	sto͞ol	Jew	/ū/
to͞ol	to͞oth	Kew	/ū/
cho͞ose	glo͞om	pew	/ū/
gro͞om	ro͞om	stew	/ū/
bro͞om	mo͞on	view	/ū/
so͞on	spo͞on	blew	/o͞o/
afterno͞on	dro͞op	drew	/o͞o/
lo͞op	tro͞op	chew	/o͞o/
bo͞ot	ro͞ot	crew	/o͞o/
sho͞ot	bo͝ok	flew	/o͞o/
bro͝ok	co͝ok	grew	/o͞o/
ho͝ok	lo͝ok	screw	/o͞o/
to͝ok	go͝od	threw	/o͞o/
sto͝od	wo͝od	knew	/ū/
fo͝ot	wo͝ol		

Like long /ō/, long /ū/ has some exceptions to 'ew' at the end of words, and that is 'ue'.

blue   clue   due   glue   sue   true

This 'ue' spelling is usually used at the *end* of words of *more than one syllable*:—

continue AA	avenue A	rescue 30
issue AA	virtue A	statue 32
value AA	pursue 49	tissue 12

Tuesday 25 (This *is* really a final spelling, because it means 'the day of Tiw'.)

Teacher's note

These polysyllabic words are for reading only at this stage, unless it is felt that the pupil can manage them. Even so, leave 'virtue' and 'pursue' until the 'ir' 'ur' spelling has been taught.

Again if 'ue' is *within* a word it splits into two syllables.

e.g.　crū/el　dū/el　desū/etude

SENTENCES FOR DICTATION

The food at school is ghastly.

Hang your coat on that hook on the door.

Put the boot on the other foot, you fool.

Shall we cool off in the rich man's pool?

I hope Liverpool wins the cup.

We may choose whatever we wish from the shop if we win the pools.

We took the troop for a walk in the woods, and came back footsore.

She is a good cook as a rule, but today the lunch went wrong.

When the moon is full, some men act the fool.

When my tooth broke, I fainted.

This is a very gloomy room.

Isn't that a new coat?

I knew she was a show-off.

Only a few of them came to lunch as the rest were ill.

Did you have a good view from the top of the hill?

The wind was so strong it blew my hat away.

I'll have some of that stew you're cooking for the crew. It smells good.

She blew all the money on food.

Brick is stronger than wood, as wood rots.

SENTENCES FOR DICTATION ('ue' finally)

When you go to the shops will you get me some blue wool?

"Give me a clue," said Sue. "Okay, it's blue," said Joe. "Then it can't be glue," said Sue.

"The rent is due," said Sue. "It can't be true," said Joe, "I only paid it the other day".

She told him she will sue him if he prints what she said.

fruit	suit	juice	bruise	cruise
biscuit	build	building	built	
through	truth	group	soup	route
Ruth	queue	sew		

MNEMONIC RHYME

(Pronounce 'fruit' etc. to rhyme with 'stew it'.)

How do you like your fruit?
Fresh? or must I stew it?
Don't spill the juice
All over poor Lewis,
It will ruin his suit
And I'll have to renew it!

SENTENCES FOR DICTATION

I hate waiting in a queue.
The truth is that the group is in the soup!
The Romans built their buildings very well. They are still standing today.
No decent builder will build a crooked building.
There are no biscuits in the place. Just as well, since biscuits make you fat!
She is not much of a cook, but she can sew very well.
I fell over and have a huge bruise on my leg.
He gave me such a huge hug that I was bruised all over.
We went on a cruise to Mexico for a holiday.
Fruit juice stains badly.
I have two brothers.
He came through the door and fell flat on the floor.

EXERCISES

SHORT FORMS

St.   = Saint   p'raps   = perhaps

St.	= Street	'plane	= aeroplane
Rd	= Road	'phone	= telephone
tho'	= though	mth	= month
thro'	= through	yr	= year

24th August is St. Bartholomew's day.

**Turn these NEGATIVE sentences into AFFIRMATIVES.
(The first has been done for you.)**
You can't row, can you?
You can row, can't you?

He didn't mow the grass. (mowed)
I wasn't going to pay him anyway. (was going)
He didn't show me those roses. (showed)
I didn't know it was snowing. (knew)

**Make these PAST CONTINUOUS by adding 'ing' to the verb,
and using the past tense of the helper verb 'to be' (the first has
been done for you):—**
It snowed.
It <u>was</u> snow<u>ing</u>.

The water flowed from the tap.
She glowed in the warmth of the fire.
He rowed very slowly.
I strained myself to catch up with the others.
The police gained on them all the time.

Now turn these back into the REGULAR PAST TENSE (-ed).
We were sailing along the coast of England.
I was gaining a stone every month.
They were waiting for the last train.
Mr. James was loading up his cart with coal.
She was sewing a new dress for her sister.
We were queuing for the cinema.
We were playing darts in the pub.

Long /ī/

Medially	List I Finally	List II Finally
'igh'	'y'	
bright	by	reply
blight	my	July
fight	cry	rely
fright	dry	occupy
flight	fly	satisfy
knight	fry	multiply
light	guy	
might	shy	
night	sly	
plight	sky	
right	spy	
sight	try	
tight	why	

Like long /o/ and long /u/, there are a few long /ī/ words which are made by adding an 'e' in the final position:—

die   lie   pie   tie

MNEMONIC RHYME ('ie' words)

He hanged himself by his tie,
What a sad way to die.
And why did he die?
Cos' he doesn't like pie,
and that's not a lie!

SEE IF YOU CAN MAKE ONE UP!

SENTENCES FOR DICTATION
Can you put off the light; it is much too bright.
The flight was delayed for two days.

Her belt is so tight it gives her a pain.

Fight for what you know is right.

What a sight it was — the stark mountains against the bright blue of the sky.

I wonder which is the right road? Tom is pretty certain this is the wrong one.

MNEMONIC RHYME

In the dark of the night,
When you wake with a fright,
And there in the gloom,
Monsters wait in your room,
Just switch on the light,
That's the end of your plight.

ODD WORDS

eye

sigh   high   thigh   height

buy   bye

SENTENCES FOR DICTATION

She gave a sigh and lay on the hay to die.

I hate these high buildings.

I must say goodbye though it makes me want to cry.

Herbert wants to buy himself a new car.

SHORT FORMS FOR INFORMATION

e.g.	= for example (exempli gratia)
etc.	= and the others, and so forth (et cetera)
i.e.	= that is (id est)
viz.	= namely (videlicet)
Co.	= Company; County
c/o	= care of
Ltd.	= Limited

mfg. = manufacturing
a.m. = before noon (ante meridiem)
p.m. = afternoon (post meridiem)

Teacher's note

It should now be explained about time being measured from the meridian line (or at midday). Some explanation will also be needed for the next two, viz. A.D. and B.C., because time runs from nought in both directions. Here too, a word about the expression 'twentieth century'.

B.C. = before Christ
A.D. = after Christ (anno domini — in the year of the Lord)
P.S. = post script, afterthought
R.S.V.P. = reply if you please (repondez s'il vous plait)
P.T.O. = Please turn over.

CAN YOU THINK OF SOME MORE?

Long /ē/

Teacher's note

Long /ē/ is the awkward one, as we have already mentioned, so we have left it till last. It has two possibilities, 'ee' and 'ea', but no guidelines as to which to use. Since e — e is such an unusual long /ē/ spelling, virtually all long /ē/ words are spelt 'ee' or 'ea'. This means there are so many of them that to list them all would be impossible. So we have decided to give a list of AA and A words which *must* be learnt because they are used so often, and a list of homophones. These, too, *must* be known, because if the wrong one is used it will change the meaning of the sentence. For the rest, now is the time to really get to know how to use a dictionary — the poor speller's best friend. Dictionary work should be included in every lesson from now on.

The pupil's visual imagery should also be built up by getting him to write the word with both spellings and asking him to decide which 'looks right'.

He can then check his decision by looking it up in the dictionary.

RHYME FOR LONG /ē/

Now comes the crunch,
Your nails you'll munch,
When choosing what to use for /ē/
For this is *really* hard to *see*.
'EE' will do, and 'EA' too,
It's all left to little you!
Look through the list of words we've set.
The common ones we know you'll get.

Long /ē/

'ee'				'ea'			
free	AA	bee	A	sea	AA	tea	A
knee	AA	coffee	A	lead	AA	cream	A
see	AA	committee	A	read	AA	steam	A
three	AA	deed	A	dream	AA	team	A
tree	AA	feed	A	stream	AA	cheap	A
agree	AA	seed	A	each	AA	leap	A
degree	AA	speed	A	reach	AA	meal	A
need	AA	sheep	A	teach	AA	steal	A
indeed	AA	asleep	A	mean	AA	conceal	A
seem	AA	cheek	A	deal	AA	speak	A
been	AA	Greek	A	real	AA	weak	A
seen	AA	heel	A	eat	AA	treat	A
green	AA	steel	A	beat	AA	treaty	A
queen	AA	wheel	A	heat	AA	repeat	A
between	AA	fleet	A	meat	AA	defeat	A
deep	AA	greet	A	seat	AA	ease	A

keep	AA	sheet	A	east	AA	disease A
sleep	AA	peer	A	least	AA	feast
week	AA	cheer	A	please	AA	breathe A
feel	AA	teeth	A	increase	AA	beneath A
feet	AA	fifteen	A	peace	AA	spear A
meet	AA	proceed	A	leave	AA	disappear A
street	AA			ear	AA	beach A
sweet	AA			dear	AA	cease A
speech	AA			fear	AA	clean A
				clean	AA	lean A
				near	AA	wheat A
				year	AA	
				appear	AA	
				hear	AA	
				reason	AA	
				season	AA	

HOMOPHONES

'ee'	'ea'	'ee'	'ea'
see	sea	tee	tea
flee	flea	beech	beach
reed	read	peek	peak
leek	leak	peel	peal
reel	real	steel	steal
been	bean	deer	dear
sheer	shear	meet	meat

HOW TO USE A DICTIONARY

This becomes a necessary part of your equipment, now that we have come to long /ē/.

All dictionaries fall into regular quartiles. If you know where these 'cut-off' points are, your search through your dictionary is cut by three-quarters.

Words beginning with letters A — E

　　　　,,　　　　,,　　　　,,　　　　,,　　F — M

　　　　,,　　　　,,　　　　,,　　　　,,　　N — S

　　　　,,　　　　,,　　　　,,　　　　,,　　T — Z

MNEMONIC SENTENCE

<u>E</u>lephants <u>M</u>ake <u>S</u>quirts

The initial letters of these words give you the three 'cut-off' points.

Now you will begin to see why your alphabet work was so important. If the word you are looking for begins with a letter between A and M, you open the dictionary at the half-way mark — this will be 'M' — now if it begins with a letter between A and E, you open it in half again — now you will be at 'E' — your pages of 'search' are reduced to a quarter of the dictionary in just a few seconds.

Using your alphabet knowledge you can always judge which quartile you will need.

Now you must train yourself to 'alphabetize' the word. This means working through the word letter by letter, using the top of the dictionary where you will see printed boldly, the first and last word on the page, and deciding whether your word is:—

a) on the page

b) before the page

c) after the page

This takes a lot of practice, so we will begin with a very simple word — PET.

Open the dictionary in the middle — does 'P' come before or after 'M'? ('M' is the middle letter, remember?) — it comes *after*.

Taking the last half of the dictionary, open this in half again. You are now at 'S'.

'P' comes in the quartile N — S

Eyes at top of page, turn back until you reach words beginning with 'P'. Now alphabetize. 'E' comes after 'A' so turn on to the page where you see 'PE' at the top. Now search for PET.

Close the dictionary, set the stop watch and look for the word 'SIMPLE'. Now try 'EXTRAORDINARY'. As you speed up, try for these time limits:—

three words per minute — up to 10 years old.

four words per minute — over 10 years old.

SENTENCES FOR DICTATION (high count words)

Most men are five feet, nine inches tall.

I fear a degree will never come within my reach.

I agree with Jane that you are very sweet.

I have been to London to see the Queen.

There are three huge trees in my brother's garden.

There are seven days in a week.

I feel weak at the knees.

My feet are killing me.

I hope Chelsea win the football cup.

The butcher in the High Street has the best meat, but he's not cheap.

Please increase my pay, or I shall have to leave.

Will you have tea or coffee?

I like cream in my coffee and milk in my tea.

This is all Greek to me.

He has a disease that makes him sleepy.

Three cheers, I see there's cheese after all.

That's no reason to disappear with my spear.

Ted made a long speech on the Treaty of Rome.

The back wheel came off when we crashed near the beach.

SENTENCES FOR DICTATION (homophones)

We can see the sea from here.

Flee from that dog, it has fleas.

There are beech trees on that hill above the beach.

That small deer over there is a dear, he will let you stroke him.

I have been to the shop to get a tin of beans.

My feet are very sore after that walking feat over hill and dale.

She wore a sheer night-dress.

He wants the shears to trim the hedge.

Take a peek at Jane in her peaked cap!

The rain water pipe leaked over the fresh leeks.

I'll meet you by the meat market.

Did you read in the Daily Mail that the reeds in that stream in Devon are dangerous?

Please peel this orange for me.

A peal of bells greeted the bride when she arrived.

Will you please get me a reel of blue silk?

Is that man real or is he made of wax?

You didn't really steal this steel, did you?

'ea' saying /ā/

ODD WORDS

great   steak   break
breakfast

SENTENCES FOR DICTATION (odd words)

Mildred gave us great big steaks for lunch.

It was a wonderful break to get away from it all.

George drove the car at breakneck speed.

The poor horse cannot break loose from this noose. It is a great shame to treat him so.

A steak costs nearly one hundred pence.

Do you like eggs for breakfast?

EXERCISES

MORE SHORT FORMS FOR INFORMATION

G.P.O.   = General Post Office.

O.H.M.S.   = On Her Majesty's Service.

H.M.S.   = Her Majesty's Steamship.
M.P.   = Member of Parliament or Military Police.
J.P.   = Justice of the Peace.
R.N.   = Royal Navy.
R.A.F.   = Royal Air Force.

WHAT ABOUT SOME MORE?

Fill in the missing long /ē/ words.
Have you paid the surgeon's _____ yet?
The _____ of this jumper are too long.
I like roast _____, but not for breakfast.
I wish I had a _____ iron for these dry clothes.
If you use _____ it makes things whiter.
She left all her things in a _____ on the floor.

VISUAL IMAGERY
Choose the correct spelling.
I (feel/feal) sick, so I'll just (leen/lean) back and close my eyes.
She is a (deer/dear) to try to (conceal/conceel) her dislike of
    his mother.
We never reached the last (tea/tee) on the golf links.
This (meet/meat) is bad, throw it away.
We had a nice (meel/meal) but I (feel/feal) sure the bill was too
    high.
Can you (reech/reach) the top of the cliff from there?
Will you please pass me the (steel/steal) rod?
Joan gave a (screem/scream) when she met the ghastly (freek/
    freak).
Do I (need/nead) to (decreese/decrease) many stitches when I get
    to the waist?
This cold (breeze/breaze) will (freeze/freaze) the lake.
The Duke of Wellington (defeeted/defeated) Napoleon at Waterloo
    in 1815.
To (meat/meet) one's Waterloo (meens/means) a final (defeat/
    defeet).

Napoleon (beat/beet) a hasty (retreet/retreat).
The swan has a very strong (beak/beek).

NOW WRITE THEM OUT!

LETTER WRITING

1. THE INFORMAL LETTER

Put your address at the TOP RIGHT HAND corner of the page, then the date below that. Starting on a line below the date, begin to write at the LEFT.

You can start with:—
Dearest Mum/Dad
Darling James/Jane
Dear John/June

Begin your letter below this opening, about an inch in from the margin. This type of letter is 'chatty', full of short forms, slang and idioms. Just as though you were talking on paper.

It can end:—
with love/best love/all my love. Then you sign your *Christian name* only.

2. THE FORMAL LETTER

This starts with your address and the date as before, but below this you put the address of the person you are writing to on the LEFT of the paper. Then begin your letter:—

Dear Mr./Mrs./Miss

Keep the language formal — no short forms or slang and end:—

'Yours sincerely' signing with your *Christian name and surname.*

'ea' saying /ĕ/

bread	steadily	breath
breast	instead	death
dead	tread	wealth
dread	heavy	wealthy
dreadful	heaven	health
lead	jealous	healthy
read	weather	stealth
ready	heather	meadow
already	leather	weapon
head	feather	threat
spread	treasure	sweat
thread	pleasure	deaf
steady	measure	deafen

ODD WORDS

bear   pear   wear   swear   whether

SENTENCES FOR DICTATION

"No more thread, no more thread," he said sadly, as he fell asleep,
    too tired and ill to care any more.

Are you deaf? I've called you twice.

What dreadful weather we are having. It is most unpleasant to
    walk up to one's knees in mud!

The Bren gun is a deadly weapon, even if it doesn't hit you in
    the head.

The poor horse was sweating under the heavy load.

The rain fell steadily all afternoon; it was as if the heavens were
    weeping.

The sheep are eating grass in the meadow.

You must do it, whether you want to or not.

If you are ready, can you go instead of me?

She is already at death's door.
Whether or not the weather is fine, we shall go for a walk through
the heather.
Shoes are made of leather — good ones, that is.
I just don't have a thing to wear.
Must you wear that ghastly coat?

EXERCISES
ANAGRAMS ('ea' saying /ĕ/)

LEATHWY	= rich
REASEPLU	= enjoyment
LOUSEJA	= envious
THEAFER	= light as a _____
EDAH	= at the _____ of the queue
SEARTRUE	= found in a chest
REAP	= fruit
REBA	= animal
FENDAE	= to make deaf
RENTEATH	= to intimidate

VOWEL DIGRAPHS

The 'come hither' sound

Medially		Finally
'oi'	*'oi'*	*'oy'*
oil	disappoint	boy
boil	choice	coy
coil	rejoice	joy
foil	voice	Roy
soil	noise	toy
spoil	poise	Troy
toil	hoist	annoy
coin	joist	convoy
join	toilet	destroy

joint	exploit	employ
disjoint	avoid	enjoy
point	poison	
appoint	ointment	

Exceptions where the 'oy' spelling comes in the middle of words instead of at the end:—

royal   loyal   oyster   voyage   Rolls Royce

MNEMONIC RHYME

Royal, loyal oysters,
Ride in Rolls Royces,
When they go on voyages.
(That's why they're so expensive!)

If the letters 'oi' are reversed the word or syllable will split into two as with previous vowel digraphs.

e.g.   lī/on   vī/olent   vī/olin   perī/od

SENTENCES FOR DICTATION

Avoid drinking poison if you want to stay alive!
Spare the rod and spoil the child.
My car needs some more oil.
That dreadful noise will deafen me.
The monster coiled his tail round the legs of the knight's horse.
We can only afford a joint of meat on Sundays.
If you toil all day in the heat, you may faint.
Put some ointment on that sore place on your elbow.
I rejoice at the approach of her footsteps.
We went in convoy to the coast.
I don't think anyone will employ him.
Do not annoy me, it is so annoying.
I do enjoy a good film.
It is wrong to exploit a child.

ANAGRAMS

NOISTIDJ = to dismember.
POISINTDAP = to upset.
PINTPOA = to give a job to someone.
PLOXITE = a deed.
STOIJ = a beam supporting the floor.
SITOH = to lift.

Fill in 'ea' and mark whether the vowel sound is long or short. (The first has been done for you.)
Have you rĕad this book? Can I rēad it next?
Do not br___the so h___vily.
I must stop to catch my br___th.
Dogs must be kept on a l___d.
L___d paint is poisonous.
Thank h___ven the w___ther is good.

Fill in the missing words (oi/oy).
Will you _____ me in a glass of beer?
The _____ in our garden is pure clay.
The _____ in the night club was deafening.
"My plans have been _____," said the villain.
It's a noisy _____ that annoys an oyster most.
The soldiers got into the town in the wooden horse of _____.
This _____ is blunt, can you sharpen it for me?
Mr. Ashcroft will not _____ Jim any more.
We have a _____ of two dishes.
She jumped for ____.

VOWEL DIGRAPHS

The 'OUCH' sound

'ou'	'ou'	'ow'	'ow'
bound	loud	bow	tower
found	shout	brow	towel

gr<u>ou</u>nd	st<u>ou</u>t	c<u>ow</u>	v<u>ow</u>el
h<u>ou</u>nd	tr<u>ou</u>t	h<u>ow</u>	p<u>ow</u>der
m<u>ou</u>nd	<u>ou</u>t	n<u>ow</u>	<u>ow</u>l
p<u>ou</u>nd	f<u>ou</u>l	r<u>ow</u>	f<u>ow</u>l
r<u>ou</u>nd	m<u>ou</u>nt	v<u>ow</u>	gr<u>ow</u>l
ar<u>ou</u>nd	am<u>ou</u>nt	all<u>ow</u>	cr<u>ow</u>d
s<u>ou</u>nd	c<u>ou</u>nt	end<u>ow</u>	cl<u>ow</u>n
w<u>ou</u>nd	acc<u>ou</u>nt	br<u>ow</u>n	
h<u>ou</u>se	c<u>ou</u>nty	cr<u>ow</u>n	
m<u>ou</u>se	ab<u>ou</u>t	d<u>ow</u>n	
<u>ou</u>r	al<u>ou</u>d	dr<u>ow</u>n	
fl<u>ou</u>r	s<u>ou</u>th	t<u>ow</u>n	
h<u>ou</u>r	m<u>ou</u>th	fl<u>ow</u>er	
s<u>ou</u>r	tr<u>ou</u>sers	p<u>ow</u>er	
cl<u>ou</u>d	n<u>ou</u>n	sh<u>ow</u>er	

Teacher's note

Suggest that the pupil takes a look at this pattern. It is not as neat as 'oi' and 'oy' but on the whole you will be safe if you choose 'ou' before 'nd' 'nt' 't' 'd' 'se' and 'th'. NEVER use 'ou' at the end of words, ALWAYS 'ow'.

PHRASES FOR DICTATION (similes)

Wise as an owl.
Slow as a tortoise.
Fast as lightening.
Sweet as a woman.
Hot as hell.
Dark as night.
Swift as an arrow.
Slow as a snail.
Loud as thunder.
Large as a whale.
Stiff as a poker.
Sound as a bell.

Strong as a lion.
Deep as a well.

PHRASES FOR DICTATION (associations)
Boats on the river.
Ships on the sea.
Cows in the meadow.
Birds in the tree.
Fruit in the orchard.
Corn in the mill.
Dew on the grass.
Wind on the hill.

**Look in your dictionary and see how many ways you can use the
words 'come' 'light' 'round' 'sound' and 'town'.**

SENTENCES FOR DICTATION ('ou' and 'ow')
The fox hounds are out on the hunt.
That tale you told me about Janet had a hint of sour grapes!
Our house is in the centre of town by the clock tower.
We got wet through in that short, sharp shower.
There are some good plays at the Round House.
We will need a pound of flour to bake these biscuits.
George gave me some pretty pink flowers.
Throw a coin in the fountain and make a wish.
His trousers are much too long, they look daft.

ODD WORDS

'ou' saying /o͞o/

coupon   wound

'ou' saying /ō/

boulder   shoulder   mouldy   soul

'ou' saying /oŏ/

could   should   would

SENTENCES FOR DICTATION (odd words)
I said I would come if I could.
That big boulder fell from the top of the mountain and squashed
   the house flat.
The knight was wounded in a fight with a mouldy monster.
You may cry on my shoulder if you want to.

EXPRESSIVE WRITING

Teacher's note

This should be well under way now that so many spelling patterns
have been mastered. However, it must always be born in mind,
that the pupil finds combining correct spelling and free writing
very difficult. It is therefore suggested that spelling is somewhat
ignored while thought sequence, narrative and conclusion are
sorted out. Some pupils have many ideas: others need much help
and encouragement.

Occasionally an entire story should be read to prompt thoughts
along set lines.

SOME TITLES
Who I Am
My Family
My Favourite T.V. Programme
N.B. Some pupils can be guided towards serial stories with a view
to setting out Project Work at a later time.

SERIAL STORY TITLES
Buried Treasure
A Surprise Parcel
A Visit to Another Planet

Other Ways of Spelling the /aw/ sound

List I	List II	
'au'	*'au'*	*'aw'*
cause	audience	claw
because	automatic	draw
pause	automobile	gnaw
applause	autograph	jaw
applaud	authentic	law
clause		paw
sauce		raw
saucer		saw
fault		flaw
laundry		straw
August		in-law
autumn		outlaw
author		shawl
haunt		lawn
Paul		yawn
launch		dawn
haul		awful
caution		awkward
auction		awe

Teacher's note

The hints on when to use 'ou' and 'ow' apply here with 'au' and 'aw'.

ODD WORDS

| oar | roar | broad | board | cupboard | sausages |
| coarse | hoarse | mauve | aunt | cauliflower | |

RHYME FOR DICTATION (association)
Draw the curtains
Close the door

Open the windows
Sweep the floor
Clear the table
Dust each chair
Wash your hands
Brush your hair.

SENTENCES FOR DICTATION

My jaw hurts from gnawing that bone.
Cats' claws are very sharp; they need cutting.
The clause in that contract is not legal.
The dog put his paw on my lap; his paws are very muddy.
There was a pause, then lots of applause.
Don't yawn, even if you are bored.
He was hung, drawn and quartered.
I must mow the lawn, but not before dawn.
Put the shawl round your shoulders.
Did you notice how awkward he was? Wasn't it awful?
The author was pleased when everyone applauded his play.
I was in awe of my aunt because she was an author.
Cauliflower smells awful.
Have some sausages for lunch.
The laundry have lost the towel, it's not my fault.
He says he saw a flying saucer last August.

SENTENCES FOR DICTATION (odd words)

He shouts so much he has made his voice hoarse.
You cannot ride that wild horse, it will bolt with you.
"My aunt has mauve hair," said Jane with awe.
We can go coarse fishing in our lake.
He is a coarse fellow with very bad manners.
Of course Jim can do it, he's a clever chap.
He has a broad back; he can take it.
We go abroad every year.

How do you ring up abroad?
How do you ring up a broad? (note difference!)
Can you help me fix this board?
Hang your things in the cupboard.
The lion gave a roar and charged the trainer.
We could row to the shore if we had some oars.
I would like a mauve dress. Mauve suits me very well.
Have you read "Travels with my Aunt"? It is very funny.
He puts sauce on everything, coarse fellow.

SENTENCES FOR DICTATION (au/aw)
The astronaut was cross because
It was not written in his clause
That he could launch his saucer from his lawn.
He gave a frown, a massive yawn.
There came an awkward pause,
Then an outburst of applause.
He jumped on board,
The crowd, it roared.
The saucer rose up light as straw
Into the August sun. He waved a paw,
(I mean a hand).
Then came a fatal flaw —
He must land —
A river broad he saw,
He splashed down safe with brakes a-squeal!
But there's no doubt it cooled his zeal.
No more did he attempt from lawn to launch,
But sat inside and grew a paunch.

ENGLISH STRUCTURE

'Not only' is always followed by 'but also'.

e.g.   I *not only* had an enormous breakfast *but also*
a huge lunch, yet I am still hungry.

Make up some sentences with 'not only' 'but also' in them.

List I	List II	List III	
fir	fur	surprise	AA
sir	burn	purpose	AA
stir	burst	purchase	AA
bird	burden	Thursday	AA
third	turn	Saturday	AA
girl	return	further	AA
swirl	church	Arthur	AA
dirt	curl	furnish	AA
flirt	furl	murder .	A
shirt	hurl	surface	A
skirt	turf	murmur	A
thirty	nurse	urge	A
thirteen	purse	disturb	47
firm	curse	surgeon	18
circle	curtain	suburb	13
circus	curve	surge	12
first	surname	urgent	7
thirst	survive	urchin	5
birth			

N.B. List III is to be given only to those pupils who can manage it. Word counts are provided for teacher's guidance.

Teacher's note

You will notice that 'ur' is a more common spelling than 'ir'; that numbers are spelt 'ir' and days 'ur'.

Refer back to page 52 for 'er' list which may need additions now.

Tutorpack Programme   Rep 3 − 37 to 3 − 47
Ens 6 − 1 7 − 3

SENTENCES FOR DICTATION
My feet are hurting. Have we got much further to go?
Unfurl the flag on the top of the church.
The two princes in the Tower of London were murdered by King
  Richard.

She went without a murmur.
We sat beside the murmuring brook.
He came to the surface for the last time.
We cannot resurface this wall with plaster, it is too bumpy.
We shall need a lot of money to furnish the flat.
Where did nurse lose her purse?
The surgeon made a mistake and cut off the wrong leg.
Surgery can be very dangerous!
Arthur sent an urgent message to George, but the urgency of it
    was lost on him. He had, sadly, already had too much to drink.
It was last Thursday that Mother came to stay.
There are thirty dirty shirts in the wash.
I like a man with a firm handshake.
She swept past with a swirl of skirt, which pleased George for he is
    a great flirt.

'ear' saying /er/

earn	research
earnest	hearse
learn	rehearse
Earl	earth
early	earthly
pearl	earthquake
pearly	heard
search	unheard

ODD WORDS

heart   hearth

SENTENCES FOR DICTATION
The early bird catches the worm.
Thy Kingdom come, thy will be done, on earth as it is in heaven.
With all my earthly goods I thee endow.

Writers and artists do not often earn much until they become well
  known.
He takes his earnings home every Friday, and gives them all to his wife.
There was an earthquake in Japan last year.
The research grant has all been used up now.
What do you think, my dear, Jane is engaged to an Earl!
What earthly use is that if she doesn't love him?
Research may find a cure for cancer.
Pearls are found in oysters.
What is meant by cultured pearls?
Pearly Kings and Queens can still be found in the East End of
  London.
Go East, Go West,
The home <u>hearth</u> is best.
My <u>heart</u> beat faster when I looked into her eyes.
The soldiers longed for their own hearths.
You must learn some words by heart.
I love you with all my heart and soul.
Do not take it so much to heart when they tease you.
Take heart, you are doing fine!
A hearse is used to take a dead person to his grave.
If you rehearse your part well, you will not make a mistake.
The gun was heard a mile away.
The teacher's voice went unheard.
It was an unheard-of thing for a nice girl to do a job in grand-
  mother's day.
Early to bed and early to rise,
Makes a man healthy, wealthy and wise.
The hearth is where the heart is.
The man who was to be hanged ate a hearty breakfast.

PROOF READING
Which of these sentences has no spelling mistakes?
I have heard about your werk.
Her skirt is too short.

She birned the milk and the taste was awful.
I must lern to work hardur.
The earth revolves once in every twenty-four hours.
She said the perl was priceless.
Tottenham Hotsper are playing on Saturday.
The police will serch for the stolen car.
There are thirty days in September.
He left me in the lirch at the church.
We can firnish the house on Hire Perchis.

Multiple Choice spellings (which is right?)
Was it a premeditated murder
                    mirder
                    merder ?

A spider in your bed is not a nice suprise
                              surprise
                              serprise ?

ANAGRAMS (all ways of spelling /er/)
NEARL   = what we should do in school.
RUNT   = go the other way.
TYRITH   = a number.
DRUMER   = to kill.
TRUDSAAY   = football day.
RATHLEY   = not to do with heaven.
STYRITH   = wanting a drink.

WRITING A BUSINESS LETTER

This kind of letter is similar to the formal letter, but you now include your reference and their reference (which is usually the
initials of the writer and his secretary) and begin with 'Dear Sir'
and end 'Yours faithfully'. The layout is like this:—

```
Your ref. MF/SP                        10 Blank St.,
Our ref.  BH/PL                        NOWHERE,
                                       Bleepshire.
                                       CD2 4YZ

                                       30.3.91
```

The Something Co. Ltd.,
No Street,
BLANKTOWN,
Bearshire.

UK5 3XX

Dear Sir,

<u>re A/C no. 46751</u>

Thank you for your letter of the 20th March in which I note that . . . etc. etc.

Yours faithfully,

Mrs. B. Hornsby

Write a letter to the National Wool Company of Great Street, Whoseton, complaining that a skirt has shrunk when washed although the label stated it was machine washable.

THE PASSIVE

The *passive voice* means that the subject of the sentence is being *acted upon* rather than *doing the acting*. It will be easier to understand if you simply think of turning the *object* into the *subject*. This transformation is used a great deal in more formal and sophisticated writing, and will be found to have many uses.

Active
The dog bit the man.

Passive
The man was bitten by the dog.

Now, if you want to add something more about the dog, it is much easier to do it if the dog is at the end of the sentence.

Compare these two forms:—

Active
The dog that belongs to Mr. Jones bit the man.

Passive
The man was bitten by the dog that belongs to Mr. Jones.

I think you will agree that the second sentence is clearer in meaning. On the other hand if you want to add something about the man, the ACTIVE is better'—

Active
The dog that belongs to Mr. Jones bit the man who lives next door.

Turn these sentences into the passive.
John broke the window.
The man built the house.
Jack drove the car.
Joan cut the cake.
He drew the picture.
I fused the lights.
We gave the game away.

Now add something to the new 'object'.
The window was broken by John in a fit of temper.

Now do the rest.

Now turn these back into the active.

He was run over by the car.

We were sent by Mr. Jones.

The window was opened by an unseen hand.

The beds were made by Jane.

The war was won by the English.

The ship was sunk by a mine.

The church bells were rung by ten men.

Composition, Précis and Comprehension Aims

Teacher's note

a) To enable the student to apply all that he has learnt about sentence structure and word order.

b) To enable the student to join sentences with conjunctions, participles etc. unaided.

c) To test the student's understanding of the text (comprehension).

d) To provide the student with practice in explaining words and phrases as they are used in the text (vocabulary).

e) To enable the student to distinguish between essential and inessential material so that he will be able to write a précis on his own.

f) To provide practice in writing simple essays which, in this section, take the form of continuation or reproduction exercises.

Give the student a passage of approximately 300 words to read. Set 10 questions for him to answer in COMPLETE SENTENCES, (comprehension). Choose 8 words from the passage for the student to replace with another word or phrase (vocabulary).

Ask the student to make short notes of essential points. Then ask him to describe the passage in NOT MORE THAN 80 WORDS (précis).

Now write an essay of 200 words to say what would have happened under different circumstances (composition).

PUNCTUATION

You now know all the punctuation marks and how they should be
used, so see if you can punctuate the following passages:—

why did they live at the bottom of a well asked alice it was a
treacle well replied the dormouse theres no such thing said alice if
you cant be civil youd better finish the story yourself replied the
dormouse please go on said alice and I wont interrupt again

(*Alice in Wonderland*)

mrs bardell said mr pickwick one morning as she finished dusting
his room your boy is taking a long time to deliver my message
its a long way to london bridge sir replied the landlady mr pickwick
was silent for a few minutes and mrs bardell went on cleaning mrs
bardell said mr pickwick do you think it costs much more to keep
two people than to keep one bless my soul mr pickwick said mrs
bardell going very red in the face for it seemed clear to her that mr
pickwick was thinking of marriage what a question to ask sir

(Longman's simplified *Pickwick Papers*)

all right if i smoke mr keith willie nodded and the sailor offered
him a cigarette thanks said willie the sailor lit his cigarette for him
then began to tell willie about his experience in new zealand
willie was glad when lieutenant adams appeared as the sky paled
he walked round the ship with willie i had a hell of a job keeping
the guards and the messenger awake willie said adams grinned
thats serious he said they didnt seem to think so adams stopped
to light a cigarette this chip he said has been in the forward action
since march 42 its been through a lot of action the men probably
think a watch in pearl harbour is foolishness

(Longman's Bridge *Caine Mutiny*)

SHORT FORMS

couldn't = could not
shouldn't = should not
wouldn't = would not

ADDING PREFIXES TO MAKE ANTONYMS

Add the prefix 'un' to these words to form antonyms (opposites)
and then use both forms in sentences:—

  e.g. kind   unkind

I always found him very kind but he was unkind to his mother.

safe	furl	healthy	ready
burden	seen	easy	clean
load	damaged	stitch	told

SUFFIXING I

| ED | ING | EN | ER | EST | IST | ISH | ABLE |
| | OUS | Y | | ET | IVE | AL | |

Note that all these endings begin with a *vowel*

RULE I

When a word has *one vowel* before a single final consonant *double
that consonant* before adding the ending:—

hŏp	hopped	hopping	hopper
shŏp	shopped	shopping	shopper
bĭg	bigger	biggest	
swĭm	swimmer	swimming	
clăp	clapped	clapping	clapper
wĭn	winner	winning	

rŭb	rubbed	rubbing	rubber
			rubbish
skĭp	skipped	skipping	skipper
wăg	wagged	wagging	
păt	patted	patting	pattable
wĕt	wetted	wetting	wetter
			wettest
thĭn	thinner	thinnest	thinnish
făt	fatter	fattest	fatten
		fatty	fattish
chŏp	chopped	chopping	chopper
skĭn	skinned	skinning	skinny
gŭm	gummed	gumming	gummy
in	innings		
Scŏt	Scottish		
pĭn	pinned	pinning	
sĭn	sinned	sinning	sinner
chăt	chatted	chatting	chatty
blŏt	blotted	blotting	blotter
căt	catty		
dŏg	doggy		

If the 'root' word is a noun underline in red.
If the 'root' word is a verb underline in green.
If the 'root' word is an adjective underline in blue.

What does it become when you add each ending?

When the vowel is *short* and by itself, this is the *only* time you have to double the last letter before adding a suffix.

If the vowel is *long* you do not double:—

clean	cleaned
cook	cooking
plain	plainer

If there is a *consonant* before the last letter, or the word already

— 140 —

ends in double letters, you do not have to double:—

fill	filled
crack	cracking
bank	banker

If the word *ends* in a long vowel you just add the ending:—

see	seeing
low	lowest
screw	screwed

SENTENCES FOR DICTATION

Her skin is like a peach but she is too skinny.

Jane can hop. In fact, she is very good at hopping.

James hopped for two miles and is the world record hopper.

This gum is very gummy; my fingers are now all gummed together.

We have a sandy cat called Brandy.

I don't like the new teacher, she is catty.

Gwen is thin, but Pam is even thinner.

Most men are too fat after forty.

This meat is very fatty.

We must fatten up the turkey for Christmas.

You chop off the king's head with a chopper, but you can ride on
   my Chopper bike!

My mother will clap if I win. There! she is already clapping.

You can come and swim in our swimming pool if you are a good
   swimmer.

Don't rub your eyes, it will make them sore.

This rubbish bin is full.

Pat bent down and patted the dog.

EXERCISES

'MINUS' WORD SUMS

Take off the prefix or suffix or both, until you get to the 'root'
word:—

e.g. reporter = report − er = report, now take off 're' and you are left with 'port'.

explained	capped
dismember	lowest
shocking	blowing
shooting	fitted
stopper	resented

Now add together:−

clean + ing = cleaning	groan + ing =
shop + ed =	ex + port + ed =
clap + er =	grip + ed =
stamp + ing =	slop + ing =
rock + et =	sweet + est =

RULE II

When a word ends in 'lazy e', drop it before adding the ending, *if the suffix begins with a vowel:−*

hōpe	hoped	hoping	
dīve	dived	diving	diver
līve	lived	living	livable
sāve	saved	saving	savable
lōve	loved	loving	lover
			lovable
wāde	waded	wading	wader
skāte	skated	skating	skater
līke	liked	liking	likable
freēze	freezing	freezer	
creāse	creased	creasing	
decreāse	decreased	decreasing	
desêrve	deserved	deserving	
resêrve	reserved	reserving	reservable

− 142 −

rīpe	ripen	riper	ripest
ūse	using	used	usable
		usual	usage
grāde	gradual	graded	grading
chāse	chased	chasing	chaser
shāre	shared	sharing	
excīte	excited	exciting	excitable
revérse	reversed	reversing	reversal
			reversible
tāke	taken	taking	taker
shāke	shaken·	shaking	shaker
wrīte	writer	writing	
pīne	pined	pining	
refūse	refused	refusing	refusal
arrīve	arrived	arriving	arrival
fāme	famous		
fīne	final	fined	
noȋse	noisy		
expĕnse	expensive		
decīde	decided	deciding	decisive
relāte	related	relating	relative
inquīre	inquired	inquiring	inquiry
pāve	paving	paved	
brāve	braver	bravest	
wīse	wiser	wisest	
hāte	hated	hating	
cāre	cared	caring	
inspīre	inspired	inspiring	
retīre	retired	retiring	
blāme	blamed	blaming	
scāre	scared	scaring	

Turn back to your list of 'lazy e' words and see if you can put
suitable endings on them — use these new words in sentences.

Underline the nouns, verbs and adjectives of the 'root' words
as before.

I hope you are well.

He is hoping to come later.

He hoped to finish early.

Can you dive?

Let's watch the diving.

He is a good diver.

Can you live in?

Grandmother has lived here for a year.

When you freeze water it turns to ice.

I must put this frozen food in the freezer.

I like a ripe plum.

The pears are ripening well in this warm weather.

We use a lot of pencils here.

That's my pencil you're using.

Is it usual to leave so early?

We used to live here.

He was graded A1.

Bill was no good; he never made the grade.

The change was gradual.

I refuse to go.

Is your refusal final?

James' horse refused the last fence.

He must retire soon, as he is past retiring age.

His wife retired last year.

She is a very shy, retiring person.

PROOF READING

What is wrong with these sentences?

I was hopping to get a letter from you.

I am hoping about on one leg.

The children had diner in the dinning room.

Why is he writting on that roten paper?

She pined up the hem of her dress.

The poor dog is pinning for his master.

I must write a letter
It will make me feel better
And while I am writing
My pen I am biting
But as it's not written
The biter is bitten
For I cannot play
Till the letter's away

EXERCISES

Choose the right word from the brackets:—
Tin used to be (mined/mind) in Devon.
She has a fine (mined/mind).
The judge (fined/find) him twenty pounds.
I cannot (fined/find) my book.
We went (passed/past) the shop.
It is half (passed/past) two.
I (passed/past) all my exams.

RULE III

When the ending begins with a consonant, like

ly   nes   ful   s   less   ment   some

KEEP THE 'e' AND JUST ADD THE ENDING:—

hope	hopes	hopeful	hopeless
lone	lonely	lonesome	
care	cares	careful	careless
age	ages	ageless	
late	lately	lateness	
safe	safely	safety	
fate	fateful		
hate	hateful		

wise	wisely	wiseness
brave	bravely	braveness
tire	tireless	tiresome
excite	excitement	
pave	pavement	
like	likely	unlikely

This rule also applies if you put two words together:—

daredevil	dateline	notebook	scarecrow
shareholder	householder	mousetrap	takeover
sometime	something	somewhere	somewhat
someone	nevertheless	baseline	baseball

COMMON FRENCH WORDS IN EVERYDAY USE

menu   chef   vin ordinaire   plât du jour

table d'hôte   à la carte   meringue   mousse

SENTENCES FOR DICTATION

We must hope for the best, but she's pretty hopeless at Maths.

He hopes to do better, so go on hoping.

Father takes care of me when Mother is away.

He is rather careful with his money, but she is too careless.

I hate school; I think it is hateful.

Jane is a hateful girl; she teases me all the time.

Don't excite the dog, or he might bite you.

The excitement was intense on the first night of the play.

We may pave the front garden to save cutting the grass.

Keep on the pavement, or you will get run over.

I am not to blame.

I get blamed for everything.

He is not blameless even if he thinks he is.

Get out your notebook and pencil.

Are you a shareholder in this Company?

Can we have a look at the menu?

What is the plât du jour?
We had better have the table d'hôte, it is cheaper than à la carte.
I will have the coffee mousse.

RULE IV

Words ending in 'ce' or 'ge' KEEP THE 'e' or change it to 'i' to keep
the 'c' or 'g' soft when it is followed by 'a' or 'o':—

peaceable	serviceable
noticeable	pronounceable
manageable	orangeade
changeable	advantageous
enlargeable	courageous
chargeable	prestigious
replaceable	outrageous

**Can you think of a prefix to put in front of any of these words to
make an antonym?**

Note that you also keep the 'e' in the following words when
adding 'ing', otherwise they would lose their medial /j/ sound:—

fringe	fringeing
singe	singeing

SENTENCES FOR DICTATION
The weather in England is very changeable at this time of year.
We must keep the number down to a manageable size.
Jane is a gorgeous blonde, but she is not very clever.
Is it noticeable that I have got thinner?
What gorgeous meringues! But I'll have the chocolate mousse.

RULE V

When a word ends in 'y', it usually changes to 'i' before adding the
ending:—

baby	babies	lady	ladies
copy	copies	army	armies
happy	happiness	heavy	heaviness
pity	pitiful	duty	dutiful
fury	furious	glory	glorious
dusty	dustier	supplý	supplier
occupý	occupied	replý	replied
relý	reliable	envy	enviable
rusty	rustiest	lusty	lustiest
pretty	prettily	ready	readily

Teacher's note

When the stress is on the *last syllable* the 'y' has a *long 'i' sound*.

ODD WORDS

busy	business	bury	burial
beauty	beautiful	pity	piteous
	miscellany	miscellaneous	

SENTENCES FOR DICTATION

This is a good, pretty baby, but all the other babies were screaming their heads off. This must be the noisiest ward in the place.

The lady in the green coat is next, so all the other ladies will have to wait.

This copy is ready — how many more copies do you want?

You need good feet to go into the army, although it is said that armies march on their tummies!

Jane is so happy now that she is engaged to Charles. Her happiness is plain for all to see.

Envy is supposed to be a deadly sin, but I am envious of her good marks in Maths.

To be good at something is very enviable.

This room is dusty, but the rest are even dustier.

Our supply of coal is very low. Mr. Black is our supplier, but he is nearly out of supplies.

Our car is pretty rusty, but I think the Smith's is the rustiest I
  have ever seen.
Joan's baby is a lusty lad. His cry is the lustiest I have ever heard.
Dad is in a fury. He is furious with all of us.
I pity John's cat, it is so thin and pitiful.
Isn't George ready yet? He would come more readily if we were
  going on holiday.

Debden Suffixing Cards (Philip & Tacy)

DIALOGUE AND REPORTED SPEECH

If you want to write about the things people say to one another,
you can either use direct dialogue or 'reported speech'.

Dialogue
"Did I do that right?" asked Jane, "I'm not too sure," replied
  Jack, "I shall have to look it up."

Reported Speech
Jane asked Jack if she had done it right. Jack replied that he was
  not really sure, and would have to look it up.

**Study the two forms carefully, decide what is different, and then
turn the following into 'reported speech'.**

"I'm beginning to understand," Gus said, "why Dad acted as he
did. He hid the will until Tom was dead, hoping we'd get all the
money then."

"Then we'll leave the gate open," Mrs. Jones said. "No use missing
any customers. You wait on anyone who comes."

"My dearest Catherine," continued Mr. Jenkins without at all listening to his daughter, "I would not for all the world be the means of hurrying you into an engagement."

RULE VI

If the ending is 'ING', however, you have to KEEP THE 'y' otherwise you would have two 'ii's' together. (This applies to 'ish' and 'ist' as well, but they are not very common endings.) Even with those odd words 'die' 'lie' and 'tie', you have to give them a 'y' if you add 'ing'.

vary	varying	fancy	fancying
baby	babyish	copy	copyist
study	studying	bury	burying
pity	pitying	reply	replying
apply	applying	cry	crying
try	trying	die	dying
lie	lying	tie	tying

SENTENCES FOR DICTATION
Do you vary your diet?
We all have varying tastes.
I fancy a good steak tonight, what about you?
He is always fancying this and that!
I think Jim is rather babyish for his age.
Can I copy the notes from your book?
James is always copying from me.
That is Dad's study, but Jane is studying in it for her exams.
You can stop pitying me now, I can spell!
Joan is a cry-baby, she never stops crying.
"Try to stop, Joan." "I am trying," she cried.
Did they reply? They are always slow in replying.
He is very busy. What is his business? He deals in miscellaneous
    items.

Where are they going to bury your father?

They are burying him at the same burial place as the rest of the family.

Shall I apply for that job? I am always applying, and never getting anywhere!

It is very trying!

That race horse is a beauty; when she moves it is a beautiful sight.

Beautiful girls are not expected to have much brain.

Turn the following reported speech back into dialogue.

She told him they had all left as it was getting so late.

He asked her how she knew that the Jones family had gone away.

He whispered that he loved her as he held her in his arms.

He screamed at her to stop, but she walked on into the path of the oncoming car.

RULE VII

If there is a *vowel* before the 'y', you KEEP THE 'y' before all suffixes:—

play	plays played playing player playable
boy	boys boyish
employ	employs employed employing employment
	employable employer
key	keys keyed keying
enjoy	enjoyed enjoying enjoyment enjoyable
stay	stayed staying stayer
buy	buying buyer

With the exception of:—

day   daily   gay   gaily   say   said

pay   paid   lay   laid

MNEMONIC FOR THE EXCEPTIONS

If you go every day,
Then you go daily.
If you're merry and gay,
Then you go gaily.
You say it today,
But you said it yesterday.
Your pay is paid on Friday,
But you spend it on Saturday.
The hen lays eggs on Sunday,
But she should have laid last Monday.

SENTENCES FOR DICTATION

Can you play bridge? Yes, I am a good player.
I am not much good at playing cards, but I can play football.
I shall have to employ a new copy typist.
Can we get one from the Employment Exchange?
Dr. Blanish is a kind, understanding employer.
Mrs. Bender is lazy and dirty. I fear she is unemployable.
I feel keyed up with excitement.
I have lost my front door key — what a disaster!
We are going to stay with Gwen in her lovely big house by the sea.
I fear we have outstayed our welcome.
We stayed with Grandma last holidays, but we are staying with
   sister Sue now.

What do these French sayings mean?

tête à tête   vis à vis
carte blanche   fait accompli
coup de grâce   à propos

**Look them up in your dictionary, then use them in sentences to
show what they mean.**

Can you think of any more?

There are also some sayings from other languages which we meet
quite often; keep a list.

PLURALS

NOTES ON PLURALS

Most nouns get their plurals by simply adding 's' — one bed, two beds — but some take 'es' and some change the last letter before adding 'es' (viz. words ending in 'y').

The words that take 'es' end in:—

ss	*x*	*ch*	*sh*
kiss	box	church	brush
kisses	boxes	churches	brushes

Some words ending in 'o' also take 'es':—

potato	hero	tomato	negro
potatoes	heroes	tomatoes	negroes

Words ending in 'f' or 'fe' usually change the 'f' to 'v' before adding 'es':—

knife	leaf	elf	wife	loaf	shelf
knives	leaves	elves	wives	loaves	shelves

Teacher's note

When 'leaf' and 'knife' are used as verbs, the third person singular simply takes 's'.

He knifes the man in the back.

He leafs through a book.

N.B.

He <u>shelves</u> the work to go out for the day.

EXERCISES

Put these sentences into the plural:—

The man wants his money.

The woman has a child.

The ox pulls the cart.

The cat chases the mouse.

My foot is hurting.
My tooth has come out.
The goose is in the paddock.
The sheep has been shorn.
The deer is in the park.
He is my brother-in-law.
A mother-in-law is often a great trial.
He will be tried by Court Martial.
Take one teaspoonful.
Get a man to put up that shelf.
Put a knife and fork on the table.
Give the girl a kiss.
Trim the bush.
He must see the church.
Put the penny in the box.
Give the lady her brush.
Get me a pint of milk and a loaf of bread.
I want a tomato.
That man is a negro and a hero too.
He has a wife.
The leaf fell from that tree.

Put these sentences into the past (irregular).
I am a good shot.
He has a bad cold.
I begin this letter 'Dear John'.
I do exactly as you tell me.
I go to see what the matter is.
I find I can no longer swim.
He drinks six pints in six minutes.
Tom throws the ball with his left hand.
The bee stings the person who steals the honey.
I feel I must sweep this room.
I shine up the silver before they come to tea.
My hand shakes so much I cannot read what I write.

I say things I do not mean.
I draw a picture of Tom.
I speak without thinking.
He leads the horse away.
He wears old clothes.
I am so tired I sink into bed.
He sleeps all day.
I bind up your wound.
I wind up this meeting.
I fling down my hat and hang up my coat.
I run to meet him when he comes home.

IRREGULAR PLURALS

man	men	foot	feet
woman	women	tooth	teeth
child	children	goose	geese
ox	oxen	sheep	sheep
mouse	mice	deer	deer

Note the following:—

brother-in-law	brothers-in-law
mother-in-law	mothers-in-law
Court Martial	Courts Martial

COLLECTIVE NOUNS

A flock of sheep
A pack of wolves
A herd of cattle
A team of horses
A swarm of bees
A shoal of fish
A troop of monkeys
A crowd of people
A pride of lions

A school (or pod) of whales
A fleet of ships
A squadron of aeroplanes
A babble of voices
The House of Commons
The House of Lords

REVISION EXERCISES

How many things can you do with this?

'The dog bites the man on the leg.'

a) pronoun replacement
b) scale it down
c) make it future
d) make it past
e) make it past continuous
f) make it present continuous
g) make it a question in three different ways
h) make it passive
i) make it a passive question
j) make it a past continuous question
k) make it a future question

Write a story entitled 'If I Had Three Wishes'.

Write a letter to your mother.

Write to the head of a school applying for the post of teacher.

Write to the bank and complain about an incorrect entry on your account.

Look up 'invertebrate' in the dictionary.

How many little words in ANNIVERSARY?

Can you spell the days of the week?

Spelling Test to be Given at End of Stage II

brain	pay	paid	stayed
Britain	said	obey	their
grow	grew	follow	know
both	though	shoe	food
view	flew	screw	blue
fruit	truth	light	eye
see	seem	sleep	each
breathe	cheer	cheese	conceal
great	wear	whether	bread
point	poison	convoy	royal
how	trousers	crowd	crown
could	bird	thirteen	birthday
Thursday	Saturday	Monday	Tuesday
early	heart	earth	heard
rubber	skinny	final	famous
lonely	fringe	relying	occupied
dying	babies	cities	daily
women	children	clothes	centre
usual	gradual	careful	excitement
orangeade	readily	glorious	beautiful
hair	high	our	busy
road	please	church	wives
moan	year	purchase	tomatoes
choose	heaven	hopped	excited
true	ground	scared	wonder

Marking note for teachers

Less than 45 — not ready for Stage III
46-59 . . . . ready to move on, re-inforcement needed.
Over 60 . . . . Excellent

Stage III

Now that we have reached Stage III we will be dealing with words of more than one syllable.

Up until now the 'root' words we have been using have been one syllable words, although we have added prefixes and suffixes to these words, or have added two one syllable words together to form 'word sums'. The last section on suffixes and plurals has been designed to lead up to this stage.

In a way, the words we will be using now are easier than one syllable words. No longer do we have to worry about adding vowel sounds. Now, vowels have a *long* or a *short* sound according to whether they are in a *closed* or an *open* syllable, and whether that syllable is in a stressed position in a word. Usually, vowels in *open* syllables (ending in a vowel) have a *long* sound, while those in *closed* syllables (ending in a consonant) have a *short* sound.

Generally speaking, English words have their *stress* on the *first* syllable, unless the word begins with a *prefix*. In words of four or more syllables there is often secondary stress on the third syllable.

The only difficulty with these words is that the final, unstressed syllable loses the precision of its pronounciation and has a schwa /ə/ quality about it, which is confusing as regards spelling.

WORDS TO PRACTISE SYLLABLE DIVISION AND STRESS MARKING

The first three have been done for you — divide the word into two syllables, closing the first syllable because the first vowel is *short*, marking the *stressed* syllable, and putting the short vowel sign '˘' over the *vowel in the stressed syllable:*—

LIST I

děn/́tist	flannel	splendid	window
măg/net	funny	trumpet	willow
in/těnd/́	tennis	velvet	follow
passage	pistol	disgust	hollow

— 158 —

infant	puppy	hiccup	shallow
pregnant	muggy	traffic	comply
seldom	dummy	contest	imply
perhaps	Mummy	cotton	sister
happen	ugly	kidnap	Mister
baggage	hungry	cutlass	master
attend	tunnel	clammy	lantern
offend	puppet	scandal	rabbit
attempt	insult	suggest	butter
cabbage	sultry	success	letter
assist	mutton	collect	stopper
gallon	button	village	pencil
lettuce	supply	fellow	rubber
ransom	muslin	yellow	rubbish
horrid	hundred	pillow	kingdom

LIST II

In these words the vowel in the *stressed* syllable is *long* and so it will be in an *open* syllable (ending in a vowel).

Divide these words into syllables, marking the stress, and the vowel in the stressed syllable with the *long* vowel sign '‾':–
The first three have been done for you.

ā/corn	pupil	slogan	lazy
hū/mid	idol	vital	agent
tor/pē/do	hero	nylon	regent
label	holy	cupid	rival
libel	student	tulip	tribal
even	open	evil	Simon
crocus	grocer	halo	Egypt
final	Peter	robot	Cyprus
decent	David	cider	silent
recent	stupid	spider	private
basin	silent	volcano	lucid
Roman	crony	poem	student

duly	pony	diet	library
duty	local	paper	primary
climax	tiger	later	uniform
crazy	vacant	ether	secret
gravy	baby	lethal	duet
Navy	lady	April	diamond
legal	pilot	chaos	diary

LIST III

Teacher's note

Not *all* words follow this nice neat pattern, however, and there are some in which the vowel is short (even in the stressed position) when there is only one consonant following the vowel. In this case, the consonant belongs to the first syllable in order to close it.

Divide these words into syllables, marking the stress and the vowels.

The first three have been done for you.

ăt/om	visit	proper	study
Brĭt/on	habit	rapid	spirit
mŏd/ern	inhabit	limit	parallel
lyric	shrivel	body	travel
rigid	magic	promise	Paris
linen	radish	determine	method
menu	punish	develop	Latin
robin	finish	envelop	livid
tenor	civic	devil	lemon
never	civil	damage	present
ever	digit	manage	triple
Helen	suburb	widow	treble
lily	vomit	shadow	select
cabin	frolic	prison	product
credit	profit	seven	level

LIST IV
WORDS WITH MIXED PATTERNS
FOR SYLLABLE DIVISION

modern	husband	public
conduct	collect	provide
confide	industry	publish
confidence	interest	pupil
congress	December	protest
connect	introduce	progress
consist	diamond	problem
contract	letter	produce
district	latter	propose
direct	later	protect
select	motor	police
divide	moment	polite
except	native	prevent
distant	notice	matter
duty	number	mater
dial	offer	sudden
effort	September	suffer
effect	over	supper
establish	remember	subject
economic	oblong	silver
electric	perfect	sister
entered	perfectly	twenty
November	open	university
together	triumph	family

LAZY 'e' WORDS FOR SYLLABLE DIVISION

a – e	*e – e*	*i – e*	*o – e*	*u – e*
invade	compete	alive	alcove	amuse
lemonade	complete	alike	propose	assume

relate	athlete	inside	remote	confuse
mistake	extreme	divide	explode	capsule
translate	concrete	polite	revoke	salute
compare	supreme	revive		contribute
welfare	delete	advise		gratitude
dictate	revere	despite		produce
brigade	interfere			introduce
	sincere			
	merely			
	adhere			

'r' as a medial consonant

Teacher's note

In words of more than one syllable 'r' no longer joins with vowels to give the special vowel-consonant digraph sounds:—

'ar'   'or'   'er'   'ir'   'ur'

Now it is just like any other consonant and has its own consonant sound /r/:—

/ă/	/ĕ/	/ĭ/	/ŏ/	/ŭ/
carry	berry	mirror	borrow	curry
Harry	cherry	chirrup	sorrow	hurry
marry	ferry	stirrup	lorry	flurry
arrive	merry	squirrel	sorry	burrow
arrest	ferret		horror	furrow
arrange	error		correct	current
carrot	terror		tomorrow	currant
parrot	errand		worry	surrender
barrack	herring		horrid	Surrey
arrow	guerrilla			
barrow				
marrow				
narrow				
quarrel				

spirit   fury   bury

You will have noticed that all these words, except the odd words, have *short* vowels followed by *double* 'rr'.

SENTENCES FOR DICTATION

The police have come to arrest you, but Harry can arrange your
   release tomorrow.
Don't carry it home Harriet, let the carrier carry it for you.
Harry is going to marry Harriet next week.
The marriage was arranged in a hurry!
The carriage on this parcel has already been paid.
The soldiers were very merry in the barracks last night.
Don't let's quarrel, life is too short for that.
We can take the ferry to Jersey, Guernsey and Sark.
We had a narrow squeak on the corner when we nearly hit the
   lorry.
I hate curry, it burns my throat.
Why are you in such a hurry?
The current was so strong she was swept out to sea.
This is a good currant cake.
Is that your current best seller?
Can I borrow the wheelbarrow until tomorrow?
I am now so clever, I can correct my work myself.
Do parrots eat carrots or do they prefer marrows?

'TION'

'ti' saying /sh/ in a final syllable

stā/tion	frăc/tion	nā/tion
elĕc/tion	relā/tion	sĕc/tion
ăc/tion	devō/tion	no/tion
fūnc/tion	mĕn/tion	tū/ĭ/tion
generā/tion	sŭc/tion	attĕn/tion

addĭ/tion	posĭ/tion	frĭc/tion
preparā/tion	trăc/tion	preposĭ/tion
ŏp/tion	perfĕc/tion	populā/tion
recĕp/tion	conversā/tion	examinā/tion
sensā/tion	inspĕc/tion	destrŭc/tion
competĭ/tion	ambĭ/tion	crea/tion
separā/tion	exclamā/tion	subscrĭp/tion
ventilā/tion	decorā/tion	composĭ/tion
dirĕc/tion	exhibĭ/tion	protĕc/tion
circulā/tion	forma/tion	quĕs/tion
considerā/tion	informā/tion	indigĕs/tion
prescrĭp/tion	mō/tion	educā/tion

Teacher's note

Where there is an 's' just before the 'tion' as in 'question', the 'ti'
says /ch/ instead of /sh/.

'x' says /gz/ instead of /ks/ before a voiced sound as in 'exa-
mination'.

'Closed' syllables have *short vowels* and 'open' syllables have
long vowels except in the case of 'i', who has now become the
tiresome one!

EXCEPTIONS

pension   tension   mansion   cushion   fashion

SENTENCES FOR DICTATION
You have a funny notion of my position in this organization.
Are you sure this prescription is for my indigestion?
You did not mention that the lotion had to be shaken.
If a fraction of your attention were given to preparation, you
    would pass the examination.
There was a reception before the exhibition.
Does the 3.30 to London stop at this station?
I like to watch Nationwide on the T.V.

What is the function of "Spaghetti Junction"?

The V.C. is the finest decoration in the world.

F.A. stands for Football Association.

All our relations are coming to lunch on Sunday.

Our expectation of success is very high.

We have no option but to sell our house.

The present generation is said to be bad at conversation.

The solution to our problem lies in your own hands.

The Princess had an invitation to the Ball.

EXERCISES

TUTORPACK PROGRAMMES   REP 3 — 48

Turn these *verbs* into *nouns* by adding 'tion' and then put them into sentences:—

to create	to prepare	to exclaim
to perfect	to compete	to examine
to separate	to destroy	to populate
to propose	to elect	to converse
to form	to inform	to direct
to prescribe	to devote	to add
to receive	to compose	to digest
to inspect	to generate	to consider

When you have written your sentences, mark the stressed syllable and the vowel in that syllable, indicating whether it is *long* or *short*.

Stress is not only important in spelling, but also in speaking and reading. If you put the stress on a different word it can change the meaning.

e.g.   We are going up the road.
          We are going up the road.

The stress would only be on 'up' if you wished to contrast it with 'down'.

Read this sentence stressing each word in turn:—

"You're barking up the wrong tree, Guv'nor".

The Syllabic "L" Family

Teacher's note

This group of polysyllabic words has a final syllable consisting of a consonant and a 'dark l', which is spelt 'le'.

A 'dark l' /ɫ/ is always used at the end of words and a 'light l' at the beginning of words. The final 'l' sounds 'dark' because the back of the tongue is raised when this sound comes at the end of words.

There are a great many words with this spelling, so, as we did with the long e's ('ee' and 'ea') we are only going to give those words with a high count to begin with.

Then there is a list of words which are *not* spelt 'le' because if they were, they would have 'non-permissible' spellings, and finally some homophones which can be spelt either way and some tiresome exceptions! In fact, this section has so many exceptions of different types that most pupils cannot grasp them all at once.

Therefore, it is suggested that the basic rule having been taught, a brief look at the non-permissable endings and homophones should be sufficient. Leave the rest for another time!

LIST I
HIGH COUNT 'le' WORDS

ble	*ple*	*dle*
table	apple	handle
stable	purple	candle
humble	simple	idle
terrible	example	needle
possible	principle	middle

ble	tle	gle
impossible	battle	angle
capable	cattle	single
responsible	settle	eagle
	little	struggle
cle	title	
uncle		*fle*
circle	*zle*	rifle
article	puzzle	

Remember to double the letter after a short vowel, unless the syllable is already closed by another consonant.

SENTENCES FOR DICTATION
Lay the table for tea.
I cannot do my Maths tables.
I will have to eat humble pie.
It does not pay to be too humble.
What a terrible mess in here!
Will it be possible for us to fit in supper as well as a film?
What an impossible task spelling is!
Is he capable of doing his homework by himself?
I am not very fond of vegetables.
A Headmaster must be a very responsible person.
Can we have apple pie for dinner?
Purple plums are the sweetest.
Spelling is quite a simple task really.
Tom is a very bad example to his playmates.
It is the principle of the thing that matters.
Handle with care!
Mind the candle does not set fire to your nightdress.
James is a very idle boy, he loafs about all day long.
I will need a needle to sew these pants.
I can't stop in the middle of a job.
All the soldiers were killed in battle.

Stables for horses
Folds for sheep
Sheds for cattle
Sties for pigs
Kennels for dogs
Nests for birds
Holes for foxes
Houses for men

RHYME FOR DICTATION

Wool from sheep
Timber from trees
Eggs from hens
Honey from bees
Milk from cows
Fodder from hay
Bread from corn
Bricks from clay

Choose a word (from 'le' list) to fill the blanks.

I cannot do a _____ one of these sums.
The _____ lives high on the mountains.
A soldier must keep his _____ clean.
Some words _____ me, I cannot make head or tail of them.
My _____ is a member of the Magic _____.

LIST II
SOME MORE SYLLABIC 'l' WORDS FOR PRACTICE

cāble	stēēple	măngle	cȳcle
fēēble	dĭmple	străngle	mirácle
bīble	pĭmple	jăngle	pártical
nĭbble	tŏpple	jĭngle	ŏbstácle
scrĭbble	crĭpple	mĭngle	treācle
bŭbble	rĭpple	shĭngle	spéctacle

rŭbble	crŭmple	gĭggle	crăckle
cŏbble	rŭmple	wĭggle	bŭckle
hŏbble	ămple	wrĭggle	fĭckle
pĕbble	sămple	bŏggle	ănkle
stŭmble	trămple	gŏggle	spārkle
rŭmble	māple	snŭggle	wrĭnkle
sĕnsible	tĭpple	būgle	knŭckle
thĭmble		jŭngle	tĭckle
nĭmble			
prŏbable			
hŏrrible			
vĭsible			

Teacher's note

'ck' is only needed on *stressed* syllables with a *short* vowel and *no other consonant* before the /k/ sound.

Think up sentences to use these words with a suitable ending added, such as 'ed' 'ing' 'er' or 's'.

LIST II (continued)

saddle	rattle	stifle	dazzle
paddle	kettle	trifle	frazzle
cradle	nettle	baffle	embezzle
ladle	brittle	raffle	drizzle
bridle	skittle	snaffle	fizzle
meddle	beetle	waffle	frizzle
poodle	throttle	sniffle	grizzle
fiddle	bottle	snuffle	sizzle
riddle	mottle	duffle	nozzle
twiddle	scuttle	muffle	sozzle
muddle	bundle	scuffle	guzzle
puddle	trundle	truffle	muzzle
cuddle			nuzzle
waddle			

muscle

castle   bristle   thistle   nestle   whistle

pēople   lĕopard

SENTENCES FOR DICTATION (List II and exceptions to 'tion')
Did you notice that the fashion writers are mentioning purple
again this year?
Poor Jane tripped over the hassock as she struggled into the pew
and broke her spectacles. It was a miracle we didn't giggle. It's
funny how one always wants to giggle in church, isn't it?
St. Bartholomew was one of the twelve apostles.
The furthermost points of the British Isles are Bishop's Rock and
Muckle Flugga. They are both lighthouses.
She tickles his fancy, so he'll wangle a cuddle if he can.
We live in the lodge at the park gates of the mansion.
I get out at Mansion House station when I go to work.
You will get a pension when you stop working.
The tension is killing me.

SENTENCES FOR DICTATION (odd words)
An acrobat has to have huge muscles.
The loafer lounged on the corner whistling at the girls.
Grasp the thistle tight and it won't sting you.
Nestle up to me and let's have a cuddle.
A man's home is his castle.
Most people like duffle coats.
A leopard cannot change its spots.
This brush has lost all its bristles.

Now you make up some sentences!

RHYME FOR DICTATION (association)
Flowers to pick
Trees to climb

Ponies to ride
Books to read
Castles to build
And kites to fly
Money to spend
And toys to buy.

double   trouble   couple   touch
nourish   flourish
young   youth   country   cousin   courage

Remember about 'o' and 'u' being good friends? Here they join together to give a short /ŭ/ sound.

SENTENCES FOR DICTATION (odd words)
Never trouble trouble till trouble troubles you.
You'd better do it double quick, or you'll be in trouble, tricky Dick.
Too many double gins bring too many double chins!
The youth of this country are well nourished these days.
Our country cousin came to stay — she is a proper country bumpkin.

EXCEPTIONS TO 'le' AT THE END OF WORDS
(non-permissible final spellings)

These words are easy to distinguish from the 'le' family because no such spelling as 'nle' 'mle' 'vle' 'wle' or 'rle' exists in English. Also, for obvious reasons, if the 'c' is soft, you cannot have 'cle', or 'sle'

dismal	cathedral	parcel	individual
decimal	central	cancel	paternal
camel	funeral	pencil	maternal
animal	several	stencil	control

signal	peril	jewel	enrol
final	April	equal	vowel
channel	rival	gradual	towel
kennel	naval	usual	original
funnel	marvel	unusual	exceptional
tunnel	novel	actual	general
panel	travel	factual	mutual
flannel	revel	manual	duel

MNEMONIC SENTENCE FOR NON-PERMISSIBLE ENDINGS

<u>S</u>o <u>M</u>any <u>N</u>uns <u>R</u>un <u>V</u>ery <u>W</u>ell.

SENTENCES FOR DICTATION

If you dial 160 in London you can hear a pop record.

Travel east, travel west, nevertheless home is best.

Is it unusual to be unable to spell?

The cathedral is in the original town centre.

Ethel Mannin's novels are about her unusual travels.

We shall have to cancel our plans to go to France this summer.

My pencil is blunt, may I have a sharpener?

A huge parcel has arrived for you — what a lovely surprise.

Cassius Clay would never fling in the towel. He has too much courage.

I can't find the towel to dry myself, as I have soap in my eyes.

General Patton was a dyslexic.

In general most people are kind and helpful.

HOMOPHONES

meddle	medal	idle	idol	bridle	bridal
peddle	pedal		principle	principal	

SENTENCES FOR DICTATION

You must not meddle in other people's affairs.

He is always meddling with something.

Tom won a medal during the war.

To be idle is to do nothing.

You worship an idol.

A bridle goes on a horse.

A bridal gown is worn by the bride.

To peddle is to sell something.

Pedals go on bicycles.

It's the principle of the thing that annoys me.

A Headmaster is the Principal of the school.

TIRESOME EXCEPTIONS – NOUNS

sandal	scandal	petal	pistol
crystal	rascal	hospital	Mabel
rebel	label	pupil	cannibal

SENTENCES FOR DICTATION

George has the sandals on the wrong feet.

It was quite a scandal when Jane ran off with Joan's husband.

The petals of this flower have turned brown.

You are not allowed to keep a pistol without a licence.

A diamond is a crystal.

There are many wards in hospitals.

That young fellow is a rebel.

You should put a label on your suitcase.

The best pupils work hardest.

Do not pull the tassel off the cord.

ADJECTIVES

local	regal	total	special
dental	sentimental	vocal	vital
mental	fatal	tribal	legal
practical	typical	topical	accidental

Now add 'ly' to these adjectives (words which describe a noun) to turn them into adverbs (words which describe a verb).

Make up a sentence using both the adjective and the adverb, wherever possible:–

He is a <u>mutual</u> friend.

We are <u>mutually</u> attracted to one another.

It is a <u>vital</u> moment in our relationship.

It is <u>vitally</u> important that we meet.

We had ice cream as a <u>special</u> treat.

Mother got it <u>specially</u> for us.

MORE EXERCISES

Turn these into past questions:—

We are finally winning.

They are equally to blame for the muddle.

James is legally the Prince.

She is exceptionally well qualified for this job.

John is mentally unstable.

Turn these back into statements:—

Were you fatally attractive?

Was Mark specially chosen?

Was she individually selected?

Were you gainfully employed?

Link these sentences with 'and' 'but' or 'so':—

She danced gracefully. She was asked to join the Royal Ballet.

Sue is gentle and pretty. She is also clever.

Robert is not a gentleman. I would rather you did not go out with
   him.

He is a rascally fellow. It would be better to refuse his invitation.

AMUSING WAYS OF EXPRESSING THINGS

**Consider these 'declensions'; they show clearly how people tend to
minimise their own faults, while emphasising those of others:—**

   I am a bit plump,
   You are fat,
   She is enormous.

I spend too much money,
You are always in debt,
They spend money like water.

I take chances,
You are careless,
They are reckless.

Can you think up some others?

MISLEADING INFORMATION (Can you put it right?)
I am a two weeks old grandfather.
The buses have decided to lay on emergency trips for the elderly
    before they go out of service.
Lewis Carrol is only a pen name, he was born Professor Dodgeson.
England collapses.
Police comb Shepherds Bush for missing girl.
Car workers drive off minister.
Mr Chamberlain makes tart reply to Mr Atlee.
Blue boy's pyjamas.
Wanted — boy for butcher.
Sale bargains — beds slashed!

**Play on words is often used in advertising and newspaper headlines,
as is unusual spelling.**

    e.g.   Beanz Meanz Heinz.
                Kleenex
                Kup Kakes.
                NE1 OU A DD?

Can you draft:—

a) a 'selling line'
b) a news headline
c) the title of a play or novel

See if you can find some unusual spellings or advertisements.

ANAGRAMS

SPITALOH	= where you go when ill.
PILUP	= found in school.
STAYCRL	= the opposite of 'clear as <u>mud</u>!'
LOSTIP	= to kill with.
TENMAL	= to do with your brain.

SUFFIXING II

This follows the same rule as *Rule I of Endings* in one syllable
words, but only if the *last syllable is stressed:* —

begín	beginner	beginning	
omít	omitted	omitting	
fulfíl	fulfilled	fulfilling	
admít	admitted	admitting	admittance
forgét	forgotten	forgetting	
occúr	occurred	occurring	
forbíd	forbidden	forbidding	
prefér	preferred	preferring	
refér	referred	referring	
regrét	regretted	regretting	
transmít	transmitted	transmitting	transmitter

If the stress changes when adding certain endings, so that *it is no
longer on the last syllable*, then the last letter will *not be doubled.*

SO	prefér	preférred	preférring
BUT	préference	préferable	

Note too that words ending in a single 'l' preceded by a single
vowel, *always double the 'l' regardless of stress.*

signal	signalling	marvel	marvellous
rebel	rebellion	control	controlled
travel	traveller	stencil	stencilling

Let's begin at the beginning.

Do not omit anything.

He omitted to inform me he was leaving.

This ticket will admit one.

Admittance is restricted to ticket holders.

Did you forget to tell him to come?

Yes, I had forgotten, I am always forgetting things.

I forbid you to leave.

Dogs are forbidden in this food store.

Our master is a very forbidding man.

I prefer to sleep alone.

He preferred Jack to Jill.

His preference is common knowledge.

The warden cannot control the traffic.

She controlled her feelings admirably.

Have you sent that signal yet?

They are signalling for help.

He is a rebel, he took part in the rebellion.

The occurrence of mistakes in our accounts is increasing.

It will not occur again.

I regret I am unable to come to your party.

I am already regretting the silly things I said last night.

ADVANCED PASSIVES

Teacher's note

These are only for advanced pupils. The answers are given after
the exercises. Occasionally give the pupil the *passive* sentence and
ask him to turn it back into the active.

Turn these sentences into the passive:—
The vandals delayed the train.

The guerrillas are hijacking the plane.

Someone has found the child the men wanted.
Someone has locked the door and we can't open it.
One expects you to be interested in your team.
People will laugh at you if you wear a hat like that.
I hate people laughing at me.
You must account for every penny.
They've asked a friend of hers to join us.
I'd like someone to read to me.
People cannot speak to me as if I were a child.
Has anyone mended that chair yet?
Someone left the light on all night.

Now use the passive form in an extended sentence.

ANSWERS

The train was delayed by the vandals.
The plane is being hijacked by the guerrillas.
The child, who was wanted by the men, has been found.
The door has been locked and cannot be opened.
You are expected to be interested in your team.
You will be laughed at if you wear a hat like that.
I hate being laughed at.
Every penny must be accounted for.
A friend of hers has been asked to join us.
I would like to be read to.
I cannot be spoken to like that.
Has that chair been mended yet?
The light was left on all night.

Teacher's note

The passive is used extensively in English for contrast, or to clarify
a point.

EXERCISES

PALINDROMES — read the same backwards as forwards.

e.g. Anna   Madam I'm Adam
Can you think of any?

Now take the following sentences, turn them into the passive and
use them in a descriptive passage, changing tense and using pronoun
replacement.

Example
The dog bit the man. (active)
The man was bitten by the dog. (passive)
   As the man crept towards the deserted house, he suddenly
felt a sharp pain in his leg. At first he thought <u>he had been
bitten by a dog</u> but on looking down he found it was a
garden rake that had sunk its teeth into him!

(descriptive passage)

Now try these:—
The man built the house.
The boy rode the bicycle.
The soldier lost the battle.
The cat chased the mouse.
The child writes a book.
The boy wins the prize.
The gun fires the shot.

**Add descriptive adjectives to the new subject
if it is felt appropriate:—**
e.g.   John got a bicycle on his birthday.
        A bicycle was given to John on his birthday.
        A fine, new, red bicycle was given to John on his birthday.

THE NEGATIVE PASSIVE

Yet another step along the road!
First turn the sentence into the passive, then make it negative.

Example

The dog bit the man. (active)

The man was bitten by the dog. (passive)

The man was not bitten by the dog. (negative passive)

(This last sentence implies that he <u>was</u> bitten by something else.)

Now try these adding a qualifying phrase:—

The man built the house.

George broke the best cup.

The nurse killed the patient.

A priest married the Prince of France.

The actress played the part of Macbeth.

Now turn the first sentence into a question:—

Example

The man wasn't bitten by the dog, was he?

No, he was bitten by a snake.

Try describing colours:—

Example

RED   — warm like the sun.

WHITE   — cold as marble, bland as milk.

Now these:—

green, pink, yellow, brown, purple, black.

These seem strange — why?

That you are early is a pity.

That you lost your purse is a shame.

How you know my name is a mystery to me.

That we haven't met before is strange.

How sugar is purified is important for us to know.

Can you make them more natural? (clue — try starting the sentence with 'It'.)

ADVANCED REPORTED SPEECH

Turn these dialogue questions into reported speech:—

Example
"Can you tell me where I can find the station?."
He asked me if I could tell him where he could find the station.

Now try these:—
"How old is she? Can she tell the time?"
"How far is it to the hospital? Can I walk, or shall I take a bus?"
"Can you count backwards?"
"Shall we meet again tomorrow? Will you remember which
  cafe it was?"
"Must we be there by seven? Can we come a bit later?"
"Must you lie around all day long?"

'our' saying /er/

Once again, this is because it is an *unstressed* final syllable:—

odour	labour	favour
flavour	glamour	honour
parlour	harbour	armour
vapour	rumour	humour
vigour	colour	behaviour
saviour	journey*	journal*

*These two have 'our' saying /er/ although it is not in the final position.

SENTENCES FOR DICTATION
Come into my parlour said the spider to the fly.
Parlour games can be great fun.
It is a labour of love.

Now put a suitable ending on these words:—

He is a man of honour, he is an honour____ man.

This pudding has no flavour, it is quite flavour____.

Armour is kept in the armour____.

He writes in a journal, he is a journal____.

She is in favour; is she your favour____ actress?

We like going on journeys, we are always journey____ from one
place to another.

Now you think of some.

ODD WORDS

court	mourn	source	course
of course	honest	amateur	courteous

SENTENCES FOR DICTATION

Manners originated at court, amongst the King's courtiers. They
were always very courteous. They never forgot their p's and
q's (their pleases and thankyous).

The Queen's house is built round a courtyard.

The court is in mourning because of the King's death.

Did you watch the T.V. play about discovering the source of the
Nile?

Our house is on the edge of the golf course.

The course of lectures is on Thursday evenings.

Of course you can come if you want to.

Do not buy a car from Mr. Lampton. He is not a very honest man.

I honestly think you would do better to go to Tom Jones.

An amateur is one who does things for the love of it, rather than
for money.

It is the work of an amateur.

**Look these words up in the dictionary and see how many different
ways you can use them.**

WRITING PLAYS

A play is usually set out in three acts, with an interval between each to allow for the sets to be changed. Each act should finish on a climax, so that people want to come back to find out what is going to happen in the next act.

A detailed description of the set is given at the beginning of each act, if possible with a sketch showing the placement of each piece of furniture and other items.

Stage directions (actor's basic movements on stage and tone of voice to be adopted) are given in brackets after the name of the person who is speaking, thus:—

Uncle Joe (crossly, as he moves up stage) What on earth do you think you are up to?
James (stepping hurriedly back and looking at his feet) I . . . I don't know Uncle.
Uncle Joe (raising arm menacingly) I'll thrash the living daylights out of you if I catch you again.
James Yes, Uncle (dashes out of the room, stage right).

Stage right and left refer to the actor's right and left when *facing* the audience.
Now you write a play.

'ch' saying /k/
(Greek origin)

Christ	school
Christmas	stomach
Christian	ache
chemist	echo
chemistry	orchestra

— 183 —

Christopher	technical
character	mechanical
chorus	architect
choir	architecture
chaos	anchor
chronicle	scheme

'que' saying /k/
(French origin)

unique	picturesque
antique	technique
oblique	grotesque
cheque	discotheque

'ch' saying /sh/
(French origin)

machine	chef
machinery	chauffeur
parachute	schedule
brochure	chateau
chassis	champagne

SENTENCES FOR DICTATION ('ch' saying /k/)

Christopher cannot come today because he has a stomach ache.

It is complete chaos in here, can't you tidy it up a bit?

What do you want for Christmas?

Christ had a wonderful character.

I want to be a chemist, but the trouble is I'm not much good at chemistry!

I hate school, it gives me a headache.

Jane is very musical, she wants to get into an orchestra.

Her brother is musical too. He has a good voice and is in the cathedral choir.

I want to do technical drawing, but because I am in the bottom
  form I am not allowed to do it.
I have a mechanical type of brain.
I would really like to be an architect, but I cannot do the maths.
Every ship must have an anchor.
This is quite a good scheme for teaching you to spell.
A chronicle is a record of events in order of time.
A chronicler is the writer of a chronicle.
Any word starting with chrono has something to do with time.

READING FOR MEANING

Fill in the missing words ('que' saying /k/):—
There is only one of these in the world, it is _____.
This piece of furniture is very old, it is an _____.
That sweet old cottage is very _____.
She is very good at acting, her _____ is perfect.
The hunchback of Notre-Dame was a _____ sight.
It is not at right angles, so it is an _____ line.
I haven't any cash, so I'll have to write a _____.
I feel like a night out, let's go to a _____.

Fill in the missing words ('ch' saying /sh/):—
The rich man has a _____ to drive him about.
The food has been rotten since the good _____ left.
The washing _____ has gone wrong again.
He came down by _____ when his plane caught fire.
The holiday _____ says we can go and live in a French _____
  for a month, and drink the wine they make there.

'ic'

Words of *more than one syllable* ending in the sound /k/ are spelt
'ic'. If you remember you were told at the beginning to start words
with 'c' and end them with 'k' until you were told otherwise.

  Well, you have been told when to start words with 'k', so now
you are being told when to end them with 'c':—

picnic	domestic	dynamic
topic	critic	hydraulic
tropic	frantic	athletic
logic	Atlantic	heroic
magic	Pacific	majestic
tragic	elastic	arctic
attic	plastic	automatic
antic	drastic	realistic
music	cosmetic	unrealistic
public	metric	fantastic
comic	arithmetic	gigantic
frolic	electric	classic
basic	cubic	mechanic
panic	supersonic	cynic
sonic		bionic

Note that when you add 'ing' or 'y' to words ending in 'ic', you have to add a 'k' to keep the 'c' hard:—

e.g   picnic   picnicking   panic   panicky

SENTENCES FOR DICTATION   ('ic')
If you sail from England to New York you cross the Atlantic.
The Pacific is on the other side of the U.S.A., the west side.
I don't understand the metric system.
He was frantic with worry all through the night.
It was a harmless frolic, but he shouldn't have done it in public.
Chopin wrote tragic music in an attic in France.
Most people in Ireland are Catholic.
I can't grasp the basic logic of arithmetic.
A cynic is a person who knows the price of everything but the
    value of nothing.

Think of antonyms (words of opposite meaning) for the following
words, either by adding a prefix or choosing another word
altogether:—

logical	elastic	realistic
attic	mechanical	gigantic
musical	automatic	classic
critical	athletic	arctic

Make up sentences in which to use your antonyms.

Add 'ing' or 'y' to the following words:—

picnic   panic   traffic   frolic

'ph' saying 'f'
(Greek origin)

physical	telephone
physician	alphabet
Philip	elephant
phrase	orphan
photograph	prophet
phase	hyphen
phenomenon	triumph
Philharmonic	paragraph
phosphate	telegraph
pharmacy	geography
pharmaceutical	graph
phonic	sphere
phony	emphasis
phantom	nephew

N.B. change of stress and pronounciation of some 'root' words when adding some suffixes or prefixes.

graph	photo
graphic	photograph
telegraph	photographer
telegraphic	photography
telegraphy	photographic

ANAGRAMS

PHAMSEISE   = to underline
RASEPH   = a short sentence
TOMNAPH   = a ghost

FORMAL AND INFORMAL REGISTERS

In the following sentences change all the first person pronouns into de-personalised abstract form.

Example
I thought it would be a good idea if we went to the concert.
It was thought to be a good idea to attend the concert.

I should know the alphabet.
I think you should start a new paragraph here.
I must have a pharmaceutical chemist on the premises of my
    pharmacy at all times.
I spell my name with a hyphen because I think it sounds better.
I don't want any emphasis placed on the fact that I am an orphan.
I think he is a phony.
I think Socrates was a great philosopher.
I understand Moses was a prophet.
I think teenagers often go through a phase of pop music.
I must rephrase that.
I must call a physician to attend Philip.
I want you to send the Daily Telegraph instead of The Times.
I think I had better forget this phrase.

'gh' saying 'f'

tough	rough	enough
laugh	cough	trough

If there is a 't' after the 'gh', however, the 'gh' is silent as in night etc.

ought	caught
bought	taught
brought	daughter
fought	naughty
sought	slaughter
thought	distraught

ODD WORDS

thorough	bough	plough	dough
laughter		draught	
dessert		desert	
Lieutenant		Colonel	
Sergeant		clerk	

ANAGRAMS 'ph'/'gh' words

RHSAEP	= part of a sentence
THGOU	= hard
UDGOH	= a baker 'needs' it
BAALTHEP	= 26 letters
WEPHNE	= aunts and uncles may have one
GHUAL	= at a joke
TMNOAPH	= ghost
GRELETPAH	= quick message

Can you replace 'get' in these sentences?
I get up in the morning.
I get dressed.
My wife gets my breakfast.
I get my things together.
I get to the bus stop and get on the bus.
When I get to work we have a get-together in the office.
I get a bit drunk and I get home late.

Can you make up some more with the word nice and try replacing it?

When I cough they laugh.

Their laughter is hurtful.

The boughs of the old tree must be cut down.

He is a good ploughman, he ploughs a nice straight furrow.

In the old days they ploughed with horses pulling the plough, now most people use a tractor.

All the horse-troughs have been removed from the High Street.

I ought to have brought some flowers for mother.

Mother brought her brother with her.

My daughter is very naughty. In fact, she is so naughty I am quite distraught.

They fought all day long, so I sent them to bed.

He sought her out in order to marry her.

These poor horses are being sent abroad to be slaughtered.

He is a thoroughly nasty boy.

The desert is hot, dry and sandy.

I want custard on my dessert.

The Colonel is dining out tonight.

The Lieutenant sent the Sergeant to drill the soldiers.

I thought I caught a cold in that draughty room.

The clerk was writing up the accounts.

THE CONDITIONAL AND CAUSE AND EFFECT

Sentences which begin with 'if' or the conditional 'should' or 'would' need to be followed by a qualifying phrase.

Finish these sentences appropriately:—
If you want me to go with you . . . . .

I would have come this morning . . . . .

We should really be doing our homework . . . . .

If I do not catch the 5.30 . . . . .

I would like to be a nurse . . . . .

If we want to watch the programme . . . . .

Look up the word 'horse' in the dictionary and see how many
ways you can use it.

Words Spelt 'ie' saying /e/

'i' before 'e' except after 'c' — think of the word 'Alice'

ie	*ie*	*ei*
thief	achieve	receive
thieves	achievement	receiver
brief	achiever	deceit
chief	field	deceitful
mischief	shield	deceiver
handkerchief	wield	ceiling
grief	yield	conceit
grieve	piece	conceive
grieving	niece	perceive
belief	priest	receipt
believe	shriek	
believing	siege	
relief	besiege	
relieve	fierce	
relieving	pierce	

ODD WORDS

science	quiet	weird
caffein	protein	seize

Some more conditional sentences to complete.
I could have passed my exams . . . . .
We would have brought some lunch . . . . .
They could have let us in . . . . .

SENTENCES FOR DICTATION ('ie' words)
The thief who robbed our house is the chief of a gang of thieves.
Make your talk as brief as possible.

Do not get into mischief.

Don't sniff, use your handkerchief.

She was stricken with grief when her daughter died.

I grieve with you in your loss.

She went on grieving about it for the rest of her life.

Do you believe in God?

No, I am a non-believer.

I heard with relief that I had passed my exams.

We must relieve the besieged soldiers in the fort.

The knights wielded shields when they fought in the field.

The fierce dog bit the priest on the leg.

His niece gave a shriek and ran to get a piece of cloth to bind it up.

You must not yield an inch.

What do you consider is your finest achievement?

The siege went on for three months.

There are too many chiefs and not enough Indians.

PROVERBS

What do they really mean?

A stitch in time saves nine.

Too many cooks spoil the broth.

Don't look a gift horse in the mouth.

A rolling stone gathers no moss.

Make hay while the sun shines.

You can't teach an old dog new tricks.

Pride comes before a fall.

Laugh and the world laughs with you, weep and you weep alone.

He who laughs last, laughs longest.

The early bird catches the worm.

Birds of a feather flock together.

If the cap fits, wear it.

The proof of the pudding is in the eating.

You can't put a wise head on young shoulders.
Discretion is the better part of valour.

Can you think of some more?

SENTENCES FOR DICTATION ('ei' and odd words)
My friend is a quiet, thoughtful person.
I have not yet received the receipt for the goods.
Seize the thief before he escapes.
It was very weird being alone in the quiet, deserted house.
Don Juan was a gay deceiver, and very conceited.
This is a high protein diet.

Words spelt 'ei' saying /ā/

eight	weight	weigh	freight
sleigh	neigh	neighbour	veil
reign	foreign	sovereign	vein
rein	heir	their	reindeer

ODD WORDS

either	neither	leisure	height
isle	island	Ireland	Irish

RHYME FOR DICTATION (association)
The lamb bleats
The wolf howls
The lion roars
The bear growls
The cock crows
The horse neighs
The duck quacks
The donkey brays.

SENTENCES FOR DICTATION
I am sorry to say I am overweight.

Queen Victoria's reign was the longest in the history of England.
Father Christmas is supposed to come on a reindeer sleigh.
You should always help your neighbour; it is only neighbourly.
Prince Charles is heir to the throne.
We will draw a veil over those mistakes!
Neither of us would be much use on a desert island.
What is the height of the average British woman?

'ti' and 'ci' saying /sh/

We have already come across 'ti' saying /sh/ in the final syllable
'tion', so this pattern is only an extension of the same idea. Here,
both 'ti' and 'ci' say /sh/:—

'ti'		'ci'	
*patient	A	special	AA
*essential	33	especially	AA
initial	13	ancient	A
*partial	9	*social	A
*influential	6	*sufficient	A
*confidential	5	*official	A
*circumstantial	2	precious	A
*torrential	0	*suspicion	28
		*politician	25
		*gracious	24
		*delicious	22
		*artificial	20
		*musician	18
		*efficient	17

Teacher's note

It will be seen that 'ci' is a more common spelling than 'ti' in these
endings. Also the 'ti' endings have a rather low word count.
However, it is extremely useful to know them because they give
helpful clues to the spelling of very common words.

Thus 'influ<u>ent</u>ial' and 'confid<u>ent</u>ial' give the clue that 'influ<u>en</u>ce' and 'confid<u>en</u>ce' are both spelt '<u>en</u>ce' and not '<u>an</u>ce', (they are both A words); and 'circumst<u>an</u>ce' (an AA word) is spelt '<u>an</u>ce' and not '<u>en</u>ce'.

EXERCISE

See if you can think of a related word to all the starred words on the list. The related word will either be the 'root' word from which the words on the list have been made, or they will have prefixes added to them to make antonyms.

Now look *your* words up in the *Thorndike Lorge Dictionary* and see what word count they have. In most cases it will be high.

Now make up sentences containing both *your* word and the word on the list.

Examples

Can you use your influence to get me a job?

You are such an influential person.

I am not a patient person, so I await your letter with impatience.

The rain came down in torrents; it was a torrential storm.

'sion'

In the final syllable 'sion' the 'si' usually has the voiced sound /zh/ as in:—

vision	*occasion*
television	decision
revision	erosion
confusion	exclusion
precision	inclusion
fusion	intrusion
division	explosion
conclusion	invasion
incision	

Teacher's note

The syllable just before the 'sion' is the *stressed* syllable in all
these words, and as it is an *open* syllable all the vowels will be
long, except tiresome 'i' again!

EXERCISES

All the above words are *nouns*. Turn them into *verbs* (which will
end in 'se' or 'de') and use both the verb and the noun in
sentences:—

Example
She does not <u>televise</u> (verb) well.
I saw her on <u>television</u> (noun).

ODD WORDS

ocean   anxious

'ssion'

If the 'si' is soft, like /sh/ the final syllable is usually spelt 'ssion'
as in

mission		*passion*
permĭssíon	ădmĭssíon	cŏmmĭssíon
ōmĭssíon	sŭbmĭssíon	sŭccéssion
cŏncéssion	ăccéssion	recĕssíon
cŏmpắssíon	prōféssion	ăggréssion
pōssĕssíon	ĭmprĕssíon	sŭpprĕssíon
rēprĕssíon	dĭscŭssíon	ĕxprĕssíon
prōcéssion	prōgrĕssíon	dīgrĕssíon

Teacher's note

In this case the vowel before the 'ssion' is, of course, short, being
followed by a double consonant. If the *first* syllable is *open* the

vowel is *long*, and if it is *closed* the vowel is *short*. These words make very good syllable division and vowel marking exercises.

EXERCISE

All the above words are *nouns*.

Turn them into *verbs* (which will end in 'it' 'eed' 'ede' or 'ss') and use both verb and noun in sentences, where possible.

Example

He wanted to <u>impress</u> me (verb).
He made a good <u>impression</u> (noun).

'i' with a /y/ sound

In these words it sounds as if there is an 'i' *and* a 'y', but this *never* happens. You can only have 'i' *or* 'y':—

million	radio	Spaniard
onion	superior	appropriate
union	inferior	experience
opinion	mysterious	audience
companion	industrious	barrier
champion	victorious	premier
dominion	warrior	alien
billion	senior	obedient
studio	immediate	studious
serious	secretarial	convenient
various	cordial	expedient
curious	brilliant	immediate
previous	radiant	glorious

EXERCISE

Make up sentences using all these words. Look them up in your dictionary if you are not sure of the meaning.

region   legion   religion   piano   idea
parliament

SENTENCES FOR DICTATION (odd words)
Religions are legion in this region.
The piano was a good idea.
He stood for parliament but he was not elected.
Can you play the guitar as well as the piano?

'ture' saying /cher/

picture	capture	fixture
creature	nature	mixture
furniture	scripture	manufacture
future	adventure	fracture
puncture	lecture	denture
culture	literature	structure

ODD WORDS

figure   failure   injure
procedure   pressure

SENTENCES FOR DICTATION
That picture is worth a million pounds.
What a boring lecture! I've heard it all before.
The Trade Unions keep on dishing up the same old mixture as before.
Her failure to repair the puncture was due to a secretarial error.
We shall need some new furniture for the studio.
It was quite an adventure when we got lost in the mysterious
    underground passages.

**Now write a story bringing in as many 'ture' words and 'i' saying
/y/ words as possible.**

fatigue	prologue	league
intrigue	epilogue	colleague
	catalogue	

ODD WORD

language
('gu' saying /gw/)

EXERCISE

How many ways can you spell these sounds?

/ch/   /j/   /zh/

'er' of the agent spelt 'or'

The most usual way of spelling the person who does something is 'er' as in:—

bake	bak<u>er</u>
teach	teach<u>er</u>

but some verbs take 'or' instead.

There is a pattern to the words that add 'or' instead of 'er' and it is that when the 'root' word ends in 'ct' 'it' 'ate' or 'ession', the 'er' of the agent is spelt

'or'

Take the following agents back to their 'root' word by removing the 'or' and see which pattern they belong to:—

Examples

objector	object	'ct'	(verb)
editor	edit	'it'	(verb)
indicator	indicate	'ate'	(noun)
successor	succession	'ession'	(noun)

State whether the 'root' word is a noun or a verb.

actor	visitor	accelerator
collector	inheritor	orator
instructor	solicitor	negotiator
inspector	educator	professor
selector	operator	aggressor
conductor	exterminator	possessor
factor	dictator	suppressor
director	imitator	repressor
tractor	radiator	processor
elector	duplicator	confessor
reflector	navigator	
extractor	inflator	
defector	calculator	

Also note:—

doctor author sailor tailor governor

mayor major minor

final /er/ spelt 'ar'

altar	burglar	vinegar	muscular
guitar	vicar	regular	singular
scholar	cigar	familiar	grammar
cellar	cigarette	peculiar	mustard
pillar	dollar	particular	custard
beggar	collar	popular	wizard

ODD WORDS

area Europe European acre

neuter neutral burial iron

SENTENCES FOR DICTATION

People in offices are white collar workers.

The word 'success' has three socks and two collars.
A dollar is American currency.
You need a solicitor if you want to buy a house.
This place is familiar; I have a feeling I have been here before.
The Swiss have always been neutral, which is why they are in such
    a good economic position.
The vicar presided at the burial in freezing weather.
An acre of land in a town costs thousands of pounds.
This is because it is more in demand than land in the country.
The area known as the City of London was almost completely
    flattened during the last war.
Are you particular about your brand of mustard?
Is this singular? No, it's plural.
Are you taking English grammar in June?

TUTORPACK PROGRAMME   ENG 9—5 9—6 (concord)

'ery' 'ary' 'ory'

'ery' is usually a suffix added to a 'root' word:—

brewer	brewery	flatter	flattery
nurse	nursery	flower	flowery
crock	crockery	grocer	grocery
stationer	stationery	bribe	bribery
discover	discovery	master	mastery
slip	slippery	machine	machinery
jewel	jewellery	join	joinery

Exceptions

   very   celery   mystery   cemetery   surgery   monastery

'ary. and 'ory' on the other hand are usually an essential part of
the 'root' word:—

January	necessary	military
February	preliminary	anniversary
estuary	ordinary	dictionary
contrary	extraordinary	library
stationary	tributary	secretary
history	story	glory
Tory	factory	lavatory
refectory	laboratory	gory

If 'ory' is used as a suffix, it is usually for the same reason as 'or' instead of 'er' as the agent of the verb:—

| anticip<u>ate</u> | anticipatory |
| or<u>ate</u> | oratory |

Invent sentences to use these words.

EXERCISES

Write a paragraph explaining exactly how to use a dictionary.

How many questions?
Read these. All of them are different, but they all come from the statement

IT IS RAINING

How many ways can you turn that into a question?

Is it raining?
Has it stopped raining?
It isn't raining, is it?
It is raining, isn't it?
It can't be raining, can it?
Is it still raining?
It isn't still raining, is it?
Did it rain yesterday?
Will it rain tomorrow?
Why is it raining?

Where is it raining?
When was it raining?
I didn't know it was raining, did you?
We need rain, don't we?
What a lot of rain we've had, haven't we?
When did it rain last?
Will it ever stop raining?
Who wants all this rain?
It's a good thing it rained, isn't it?

Now you try 'the sun is shining'

HOMOPHONES

be	bee	brooch	broach
see	sea	steak	stake
tee	tea	great	grate
flee	flea	past	passed
leek	leak	mind	mined
steel	steal	find	fined
reed	read	groan	grown
heel	heal	aloud	allowed
reel	real	stationery	stationary
stair	stare	principle	principal
pail	pale	to too	two
tail	tale	for four	fore
here	hear	poor pour	paw
fur	fir	pair pair	pare
saw	sore	there their	they're
sure	shore	rain rein	reign
more	moor	road rode	rowed
maid	made	veil	vale
air	heir	sleigh	slay
our	hour	stayed	staid

sent	scent	weigh	way
seen	scene	weather	whether
one	won	where	wear
son	sun	tents	tense
none	nun	prints	prince
isle	aisle	nit	knit
shoot	shute	no	know
wood	would	idle	idol
yoke	yolk	fare	fair
night	knight	bridal	bridle
write	right	peddle	pedal
week	weak	meddle	medal
hole	whole	neigh	nay
piece	peace	war	wore
waist	waste	warn	worn
male	mail	hare	hair
course	coarse		
hoarse	horse	bear	bare
new	knew	flower	flour

SPELLING FOR MEANING

Fill in the missing words (homophones):—

We went ___ Buckingham Palace to ____ the Queen.

I have had ____ much to eat.

What did you have _____ dinner.

One, two, three, _____, five.

The man was so _____ he couldn't buy anything to eat.

Will you _____ the tea or shall I?

My dog has hurt his _____.

I need some _____ slippers.

I _____ her a long time ago.

How many _____ in a day?

This is _____ house, where is yours?

The _____ fell heavily all day.

You must hold the horse's _____.
The Queen began her _____ in 1953.
Her face was _____ with fright.
Fill the _____ with water.
Cinderella is a fairy _____.
The dog wagged his _____.
—————— is what animals wear to keep them warm.
_____ trees are evergreen.
Prince Charles is the _____ to the throne.
I must get some fresh _____.
The _____ and the tortoise had a race.
I don't like long _____ on men.
Will you read _____ to me please?
Are we _____ to go out on our own?
I hope the _____ will be fine for our picnic.
You have got to do it _____ you want to or not.
Would you cut me a _____ of cake?
I want some _____ and quiet when I'm tired.
What shall I _____ to the party?
_____ shall we go for our holiday?

SILENT LETTERS

gnat	whom	sword
gnaw	whose	answer
gnu	whole	Wednesday
gnash	autumn	often
gnome	condemn	listen
sign	solemn	science
design	column	scene
align	exhibit	scent
alignment	exhaust	ascend
consign	Thames	descend
consignment	limb	indict
calm	lamb	mortgage

palm	comb	fatigue
calf	crumb	intrigue
half	numb	catalogue
folk	thumb	prologue
yolk	plumber	dialogue
psalm	tomb	colleague
almond	debt	league
iron	doubt	epilogue
write	subtle	whisk
writer	knack	whisky
wrought	knapsack	whirl
wrinkle	knob	whisper
wring	knock	whither
wrong	knot	Whitsun
who	knuckle	whistle

RHYME FOR DICTATION

I'm a G-nu
I'm a G-nu
The nicest G-natured creature in the zoo.
How d'you do?
You really ought to K-now W-ho's W-ho!
I'm a G-nu,
Spelt G N U,
I'm not a camel or a kangaroo,
So let me introduce,
I'm neither man nor moose,
G-no! G-no! G-no!
I'm a G-nu.

I'm a G-nu
I'm a G-nu
A G-nother G-nu,
I wish I could G-nash my teeth at you.
I'm a G-nu,

How d'you do?
You really ought to K-now W-ho's W-ho.
I'm a G-nu
Spelt G N U,
Call me a bison or an okapi
and I'll sue.
Nor am I in the least
Like that dreadful hartebeest,
G-no! G-no! G-no!
I'm a G-nu!

by kind permission of the late Michael Flanders

COUNTRIES

Names of countries ending in an /er/ sound are usually spelt with a final 'a':—

America	China	Persia
Africa	Corsica	Prussia
Algeria	Czechoslovakia	Rhodesia
Argentina	India	Russia
Asia	Jamaica	Rumania
Australia	Kenya	Sardinia
Austria	Korea	Scandinavia
Bermuda	Malta	Tonga
Botswana	Madeira	Uganda
Bulgaria	Majorca	Syria
Burma	Nigeria	Yugoslavia
Canada	Panama	Zambia

Who lives where?
The English live in _____.
The _____ live in Denmark.
The Scots live in _____.
The _____ live in Ireland.

The Welsh live in _____.
The Finns live in _____.
The Swedes live in _____.
The _____ live in France.
The _____ live in Germany.
The _____ live in Italy.
The Spaniards live in _____.
The Portuguese live in _____.
The _____ live in Holland.
The Americans live in _____.
The Canadians live in _____.
The Australians live in _____.
The Egyptians live in _____.
The _____ live in Israel.
The _____ live in Austria.
The Belgians live in _____.
The Russians live in _____.
The Chinese live in _____.

GIRL'S NAMES

These also are usually spelt with a final 'a' when they end in an /er/ sound:—

Amanda	Fenella	Mona
Agatha	Fiona	Matilda
Angela	Flora	Melissa
Anthea	Freda	Miranda
Alexandra	Francesca	Monica
Anna	Gloria	Moira
Barbara	Georgina	Marcia
Brenda	Greta	Nora
Belinda	Glenda	Olga
Cilla	Hilda	Ophelia
Camilla	Henrietta	Pamela
Cinderella	Helga	Prunella

Clara	Julia	Priscilla
Cynthia	Joanna	Patricia
Diana	Laura	Rebecca
Dora	Leila	Sara
Edna	Lavinia	Stella
Elsa	Lucinda	Sylvia
Eva	Lydia	Sheila
Eliza	Lorna	Sonia
Rita	Stella	Thora
Tina	Titania	Teresa
Ursula	Vanessa	Vera
Veronica	Victoria	Wanda

ODD WORDS

extra	opera	banana
panda	pyjama	umbrella
lama	cinema	camera
soda	china (cup)	panama (hat)

Write an essay entitled "The Horse, and its effect on the history of man".

BOY'S NAMES

Adam	Edward	Keith	Rex
Adrian	Eric	Kit	Reginald
Alan	Ernest	Lawrence	Robert
Albert	Ethelred	Leonard	Robin
Alfred	Felix	Lester	Roger
Alexander	Francis	Lewis	Ronald
Algernon	Frank	Luke	Ross
Andrew	Frederick	Mark	Roy
Angus	George	Martin	Rupert

Anthony	Geoffrey	Matthew	Sherlock
Archibald	Gerald	Max	Sidney
Arthur	Godfrey	Michael	Simon
Arnold	Gordon	Miles	Steven
Augustus	Graham	Morgan	Stuart
Bruce	Gregory	Nicholas	Thomas
Charles	Guy	Noel	Timothy
Christopher	Harold	Norman	Trevor
Clifford	Henry	Oliver	Vernon
Clive	Humphrey	Owen	Victor
Colin	Jack	Patrick	Vincent
Cuthbert	James	Paul	Wallace
David	John	Peter	Walter
Daniel	Justin	Philip	Warren
Derek	Kenneth	Ralph	Wilfred
Duncan	Kim	Randolph	William
Douglas	Kevin	Raymond	Winston

SURNAMES

Many people were named after their occupations, such as SMITH or BAKER.

Others added a prefix or suffix to their Christian names to denote 'SON OF':—

Johnson	= (son of John) — English
Jackson	= (son of Jack) — "
Jones	= (son of John) — Welsh
O'Connor	= (son of Connor) — Irish
MacDougal	= (son of Dougal) — Scotch
Fitzroy	= (illegitimate sons of Kings or Princes)

ADVANCED PREFIXES AND SUFFIXES

PREFIXES

a	— without, none	inter	— between
ante	— before	iso	— equal
anti	— against	mal	— bad
centi	— hundred	manu	— hand
chromo	— colour	mega	— large
circum	— around	micro	— small
co	— together	multi	— many
contra	— against	no	— not
demi	— half	omni	— all
hemi	— half	photo	— light
homo	— same	pseudo	— false
hydro	— of water	retro	— backwards
hyper	— too much	sub	— under
hypo	— too little	super	— above
intra	— within	ultra	— extreme

SUFFIXES

dom	— a quality
gram	— written, drawn
graph	— that which is written
ine	— pertaining to
ior	— comparative degree (superior)
ise	— condition
itis	— inflamation
phobia	— horror

The prefixes and suffixes can help you to find out what words mean:—

multi-storey   = many storeys

photophobia	= fear of light
pseudonym	= false name
hyperactive	= too active
subnormal	= below normal

Thus even young pupils can use these effectively.

DICTATION

Using all spellings learnt

It was a dark, dismal, dreary night when Jill and her brother
Dick set out on the thirty odd miles of rough road that divided
their farm from their uncle's. The rain had been coming down
steadily all day, and now the track was a sea of mud. They passed
an old shepherd threading his way between the puddles, but after
that the silence was complete apart from the occasional hoot of an
owl. Suddenly Jill's horse slipped, lost his balance, and went down
on both knees. Jill shot over his head and landed heavily on her
shoulder. The horse neighed piteously, but Jill lay still and silent.
Dick dismounted and hurried to the girl's side, not knowing what
he might find. He turned her over and when he saw her white face
he thought she was going to die. Cradling her in his arms he huddled
under the hedge for protection, and waited for the dawn. At last
a faint glow showed in the east, and the first ploughman came
plodding by. He turned and came towards them — they were
saved! As the noises of the approaching day brought joy to their
hearts and warmth to their bones Jill and Dick were on their way
to safety in the farmer's cart.

WORDS INVOLVING LATIN AND GREEK PREFIXES AND SUFFIXES

subtract	hemisphere
subterranean	hemianopia
subway	hemiplegia
subnormal	demi-god

pneumonia
pneumatic
super star
supersonic
claustrophobia
pseudogothic
pseudoneolithic
hypertension
hydrofoil
hydrogen
hydraulic
homogeneous
homosexual
heterosexual
hypothermia
contrary
contradictory
centigrade
centimetre
anteroom
manuscript
antecedent
postwar
postnatal

semi-demi-
quaver
omnibus
figurine
telegraph
ultra-modern
retrograde
retrospect
isotope
isosceles triangle
malformed
maladjusted
manual
amanuensis
macrocephaly
microscope
megaton
multi-purpose
coordinate
cooperate
kingdom
freedom
chronological
chronic

inter-office communication
inter-disciplinary approach
intramural (included within the college)
intravenous (within, or introduced into, a vein)

HINTS ON WRITING ESSAYS AND EXAMS

1) Read the title or question carefully.
   What kind of treatment is called for?

Exam questions often include such words as 'analyse', 'discuss', 'explain', 'outline', 'contrast and compare'.
Make sure you do what you are asked.

2) School homework essays, on the other hand are often 'a review of the literature' or 'history topic' etc.
Collect all the necessary materials — books, pens, pencils, paints etc.
Now *plan an outline*
   a) Introduction — perhaps commenting on the title, and stating what you consider the question to be!
   b) Development of main ideas, and notes on how you will support them. Illustrate with diagrams or maps where appropriate.
   c) Conclusion — a final summing up and your own opinions on the matter.

3) In an exam it is essential to answer *all the questions asked for.* Only a certain number of marks can be given for any one question no matter how well it is done, and an unanswered question is a total loss. *So time yourself carefully and allow an exact amount of time for each question.*

4) If you quote, do it accurately and use inverted commas, citing the reference with date and author's name. If you cannot remember the actual words, use phrasing such as "Professor Blank mentions the fact that . . ." or "it is thought by Dr. Nobody that . . .". In a learned paper a bibliography is given at the end.

5) *Check your essay* — have you answered the question?
Have you covered the main points and supported your arguments?
If you have time check your essay for spelling and punctuation errors.
Have you written what you actually meant?
Do you mean what you have written?

6) Take care with writing and setting out your work — *examiners tire easily too!*

READING FOR DIFFERENT PURPOSES

For pleasure
Try to 'skim' as it is not necessary to read every word of a novel.

To learn
Examine title page, list of contents, then ask yourself if you need to read the whole book.
Decide if you can skip a chapter.
Decide if there is any one chapter that will need extra attention.
Now flick through the whole book, looking at chapter-headings, diagrams and pictures and last sentences of chapters, which often contain a summary.
Now read the chapters you think need special attention, making notes as you go.
Do not skip diagrams, maps and pictures. They are there to clarify a point.
Use a dictionary to improve vocabulary, making a note of new words and what they mean.

Spelling Test to be Given at End of Stage III

dial	offer	September
family	marry	mirror
perfection	pension	cushion
vegetable	single	uncle
double	animal	decimal
occurred	admittance	because
autumn	straw	favourite
honest	journey	Christmas
machine	parachute	Atlantic
automatic	telephone	sphere
enough	laugh	ought
grief	believe	friend
Ireland	patient	ancient
ocean	revision	occasion
million	union	appropriate
secretarial	failure	lecture
author	accelerator	Europe
area	acre	grocery
February	history	psalm
whisper	yolk	limb
December	omission	court
surrender	religion	cheque
examination	fixture	logical
castle	vinegar	cough
beginning	slippery	thorough
aunt	Thames	either
honour	china	special
ache	pupil	procession
Pacific	merry	Parliament
graph	table	fatigue
daughter	people	custard
sovereign	rebellion	January
precious	awful	Wednesday

Marking note for teachers
55 = Pass

CONCLUSION

It is estimated that the following spelling ages will be reached at the end of each stage:—

Stage I — between 7-8 years, if no spelling age at all exists at the start of the programme. If it does, this stage will act as a reinforcer and a higher spelling age will result.

Reading ages are usually in advance of spelling ages, but the reading age at the end of Stage I will also depend on whether a scorable reading age existed at the start of the programme.

Stage II — between 11-12 years.
Reading should by now be both fluent and accurate, and a reading age of 12 should have been achieved.

At the end of this stage most linguistic transformations should have been mastered, and a start made on writing in the formal register. Expressive writing should also be under way.

Stage III — between 13-15 years for both reading and spelling. The finer points of literary style will have been explained to pupils needing them, and all linguistic transformations mastered.

Of course, younger children will not be expected to complete all three stages and will cease when their reading and spelling has reached chronological age. They will continue to need extra help in English at school, however, until the end of their conventional schooling.

This programme is by no means complete, but it is hoped it will prove useful to all those with reading and spelling problems.

APPENDIX I

List of Suitable Books for Reading

Royal Road Readers, Companions and Miniatures, by Daniels & Diack: Hart-Davis.
  R.A. (reading age) 5-9. I.A. (interest age) 6-9.
Tempo Books 1-10: Longman.
  R.A. 6-8. I.A. 10 and up.
Tim's Gang Books: Hamish Hamilton.
  R.A. 7 and up. I.A. 10 and up.
  (recommended for culturally deprived)
Trend Series: Ginn & Co.
  R.A. 7-11. I.A. 10-15.
English Picture Readers, The World's Great Stories and Pictorial Classics: Oxford University Press.
  R.A. 7 and up. I.A. 7 and up.
Stories for Today (1st and 2nd Series):
  Heinemann Educational Books.
  R.A. 7-9. I.A. 12 and up.
Dragon Pirate Books & Griffin Pirate Books:
  E. J. Arnold.
  R.A. 7 and up. I.A. 8½ and up.
Nipper Books: Macmillan & Co.
  R.A. 6-8. I.A. 6-10.
  (recommended for culturally deprived)
Sounds Travel Too Books 1-4, by Sonia Machanick.
  Heinemann Educational Books.
  R.A. 5-8. I.A. 5-10.
They Were First: Oliver & Boyd.
  R.A. 7 and up. I.A. up to adult.
Reader's Digest Readers: Reader's Digest.
  R.A. 7-9. I.A. adult.
Inner Ring (3 series): Ernest Benn.
  R.A. 7-13. I.A. up to 15

R.A. 7+ I.A. 12-adult.

Nelson Elementary Readers: Nelson.

R.A. 9+ I.A. 9-16.

Jim Hunter Books: Methuen.

R.A. 7+ I.A. 13+.

Tim and the Hidden People: E.J. Arnold.

R.A. 8 I.A. 10-14.

Catching Crooks — Good Detective Guide: Usborne.

R.A. 8+ I.A. 8-14.

Sullivan Programmed Readers 1-24:
McGraw-Hill.

Topliners: Macmillan Educational.

R.A. 10+ I.A. teenage.

Crown Street Kings: Macmillan.

R.A. 7-8. I.A. 12-16.

Let's Find Out: F. Watts.

R.A. 7-8. I.A. 8-11.

Let's Read and Find out Science: A & C Black.

R.A. 7-9. I.A. 8-13.

Adventures in Space: Hart-Davis.

R.A. 8-9 I.A. 10-14.

Great Battles of the World: Longman.

R.A. 8-9. I.A. 8-14.

Waxwell Books: Grail.

R.A. 7. I.A. adult.

Instant Readers and *Booster Books*: Heinemann Educational Books.

R.A. 8-9. I.A. 9-16.

True Adventure: Blackie & Sons.

R.A. 9. I.A. 9-16.

Rescue Reading: Ginn.

R.A. 6-9. I.A. 7-14.

Inswingers: Hulton.

R.A. 7-9. I.A. 12-16 (soccer, of particular interest to teenage boys).

Macdonald Starters: Macdonald Educational.

R.A. 6+ I.A. 7-9

Macdonald's First Library: Macdonald Educational.
R.A. 6+ I.A. 8-10.
Ulverscroft Large Print Series: Ulverscroft.
R.A. 9+ I.A. adult (250 titles).
Hutchinson's Educational Books: Hutchinson.
R.A. 12+ I.A. 12-adult.
Bull's Eye Series: Hutchinson.
R.A. 9+ I.A. 12-adult.
Colour Story Reading Books: Nelson.
R.A. 4-6. I.A. 6-8.
Pleasant Books in Easy English: Longman.
R.A. 10+ I.A. adult.
Longman's Structural Readers: Longman.
R.A. 8-15 I.A. up to adult.
Longman's Graded Supplementary Readers: Longman.
R.A. 8-15 I.A. up to adult.
Longman's Simplified English Series: Longman.
R.A. 9+ I.A. adult.
Longman's Bridge Series: Longman.
R.A. 12 I.A. adult.
New Method Supplementary Readers Stages 1-7: Longman.
R.A. 8-9. I.A. 7 to adult.
Ladybird Books, General Knowledge Series:
Wills & Hepworth.
R.A. 7+ I.A. 8-15.
Heinemann Guided Readers (4 grades: Beginner, Elementary,
Intermediate, Upper): Heinemann Educational Books.
R.A. 8-15. I.A. 12-adult.
Pic Papers: Kingswood Publications.
R.A. 7½ and up. I.A. teenage.
Picture Puffin Books: Penguin.
R.A. 6-7. I.A. 8-10.
Spiral Readers: Hutchinson and ILEA.

Reading ages are only suggested

APPENDIX II

Games, Equipment and Workbooks

Workbooks

Read Write and Spell, books I II III & IV by Gill Nettle and Julia Leach: Heinemann Educational.

Space to Spell and *More Space to Spell* by Frula Shear, Diana Targett and Judith Raines: Better Books, 15A Chelsea Road Bath BA1 5RA.

Oxford Junior Workbooks: Oxford University Press.

Ginnes' Phonic Workbooks: Ginn & Co.

Solving Language Difficulties: Better Books.

Spell of Words & Spell Bound: Better Books.

Writing is for Reading by Jane Taylor MBAOT., DipEd: Dyslexia Clinic, Bart's.

Nelson Handwriting: Thomas Nelson.

Gross Motor Development Exercises: by Hazel McKay: Dyslexia Clinic, Barts.

The Vowel Crowd by Jeremy Long and Jane Rogers: Heinemann Educational.

Equipment

'Salva' by Mr Eric Atkinson: See and Learn Ltd., Hill View, Walsworth, Sandhurst Lane, Sandhurst, Gloucester.

Language Master: Bell & Howell.

Edith Norrie Letter case: Helen Arkell Dyslexia Centre, 14 Crondace Rd, London, SW6.

Dyslexia, A Language Course for Teachers and Learners: Miss Kathleen Hickey, 3 Montague Rd, London SW19.

ASTON INDEX: LDA, Wisbech, Cambs PE13 2AX.

Stott Programmed Reading Kit: Holmes McDougall, Edinburgh.

Scott-Foresman Reading Kit: 32, West Street, Brighton, Sussex.

Attack-A-Track by Lynn Lewis: Better Books.

Blank Playing Cards: Waddingtons Playing Card Co., Leeds.

Plastic Pencil Grips: Task Master Ltd., Leicester.

S.R.A.: Reading Road, Henley-on-Thames, Oxon RG9 1EW.

Games

Lexicon

Snakes & ladders

Wooden Alphabet letters: Goodwood Play Things Ltd., Lavant, Chichester, Sussex.

Pictograms System: Pictogram Supplies, Barton, Cambridge.

Dictionaries

The Thorndike Junior Illustrated Dictionary: London University Press.

Spelling and Word Division 60,000 Words: Collins Gem Dictionary.

The Word Hunters Companion — A First Thesaurus: Blackwell.

Suppliers of Learning Materials

Philograph Publications Ltd., North Way, Andover, Hants.

Galt Toys, Cheadle, Cheshire.

LDA Wisbech, Cambs.

M.B. Key to Learning, Church Walk, Kings' Cliffe, Peterborough PE8 6XD.

APPENDIX III

Rhymes For Days of the Week

Solomon Grundy,
Born on a Monday,
Christened on Tuesday,
Married on Wednesday,
Took ill on Thursday,
Worse on Friday,
Died on Saturday,
Buried on Sunday,
This is the end of Solomon Grundy.

Monday's child is fair of face,
Tuesday's child is full of grace,
Wednesday's child is full of woe,
Thursday's child has far to go,
Friday's child is loving and giving,
Saturday's child works hard for his living,
But the child that is born on the Sabbath day
Is bonny, blithe, good and gay.

The Gas Man Cometh

It was on the Monday morning
The gas man came to call
The gas tap wouldn't turn
I wasn't getting gas at all
He tore out all the skirting boards
To try and find the main
So we had to call the carpenter
To put them back again.
Oh, it all makes work for
The working man to do!

It was on the Tuesday morning
The carpenter came round

He hammered and he chiselled
And he said "Look what I've found
Yer joists are full of dry rot
But I'll put them all ter rights"
Then he nailed right thro' a cable
And out went all the lights.
Oh, it all makes work for
The working man to do!

It was on a Wednesday morning
The electrician came
He called me Mr. Sanderson
Which isn't quite the name
He couldn't reach the fuse box
Without standing on the bin
And his foot went thro' a window
So I called the glazier in.
Oh, it all makes work for
The working man to do!

It was on the Thursday morning
The glazier came along
With his blow torch and his putty
And his merry glazier song
He put another pane in
It took no time at all
But I had to get the painter in
To come and paint the wall.
Oh, it all makes work for
The working man to do!

It was on the Friday morning
The painter made a start
With overcoat and undercoat
He painted every part
Every nook and cranny
But I found when he was gone

He'd painted over the gas tap
And I couldn't turn it on.
Oh, it all makes work for
The working man to do!

On Saturday and Sunday
They do not work at all
So it was on the Monday morning
That the gas man came to call

Months of the Year

Dirty days hath September
April, June and November,
All the rest have thirty-one
Without a blessed gleam of sun.
If any month had two and thirty
They'd be just as wet and twice as dirty.

By courtesy of John Barley

* * *

January brings the snow
Makes your feet and fingers glow
February nice and sweet
Freeze the toes right off your feet
Welcome March with wintry wind
Would thou wert not so unkind
April brings the sweet spring showers
On and on for hours and hours
Here is dear and kindly May
Frost by night and hail by day

June just rains and never stops
Thirty days and spoils the crops
In July the sun is hot
Is it shining? No, it's not!
August dank, and cold and wet
Brings more rain than any yet
Bleak September's mist and mud
Is enough to chill the blood
Then in October comes the gale
Wind and slush and rain and hail
Dark November brings the fog
Should not do it to a dog
Breezy wet December then —
Bloody January again!

Parts of Speech

Every name is called a noun
As 'field' and 'fountain', 'street' and 'town'.
In place of noun the pronoun stands
As 'he' and 'she' can clap 'their' hands.
The adjective describes a thing
As 'magic' wand or 'bridal' ring.
The verb means action — something done
To 'read' and 'write' and 'jump' and 'run'.
How things are done the adverb tells
As 'quickly', 'slowly', 'badly', 'well'.
The preposition shows relation
As 'in' the street or 'at' the station.
Conjunctions join in many ways
Sentences, words or phrase and phrase.
The exclamation cries out "Hark, I need a very special mark!"

Hints on Pronunciation For Foreigners

I take it you already know
Of tough and bough and cough and dough?
Others may stumble, but not you
On hiccough, thorough, laugh and through?
Well done! And now you wish perhaps
To learn of less familiar traps?

Beware of heard, a dreadful word
That looks like beard and sounds like bird.
And dead: it's said like bed, not bead —
For goodness sake don't call it 'deed'!
Watch out for meat and great and threat,
They rhyme with suite and straight and debt.

A moth is not a moth in mother
Nor both in bother, broth in brother,
And here is not a match for there
Nor dear and fear for bear and pear,
And then there's dose and rose and lose —
Just look them up — and goose and choose.

And cork and work and card and ward,
And font and front and word and sword,
And do and go and thwart and cart —
Come, come, I've hardly made a start!
A dreadful language? Man alive,
I'd mastered it when I was five.

by
T.S.W.

Index